First published in England 1980 by
Leader Books Ltd.,
Unit 3, Park Works,
Kingsley, Hampshire.


Text © 1980 Marc Alexander
Photographs © 1980 Graham & Jaquie Sergeant.

ISBN 0 907159 00 1

Printed in England by Arrowhead Publishing Ltd.

# The dance goes on

THE LIFE AND ART OF
ELIZABETH TWISTINGTON HIGGINS MBE

## by Marc Alexander

Photographs by Graham and Jacquie Sergeant

with a foreword by

## HRH Prince Philip, Duke of Edinburgh

Leader Books

## Captions to Colour Plates

## Acknowledgements

The author wishes to thank most sincerely the many people who have generously assisted him in the preparation of this book, in particular, Doug Adams, Colin Dann, Chairman of the Aidis Trust Toyaids Project, Rosemary Howard, A.G.Jefcoate, Chairman of the Aidis Trust, Sheila Large, Matron Margery Ling and Sheridan Russell. He also wishes to express his gratitude to Elizabeth.

Graham and Jacquie Sergeant took the colour and contempory monochrome photographs. Among the pictures illustrating the earlier part of Elizabeth's life are photographs taken by Geoff Baker, Les Brand, Nem Elliott, the Keystone Press, Betty Price, Peter Russell, Merlyn Severn, David Trounce, Ian Twistington Higgins, Thomas Twistington Higgins and Tony Tween.

The drawings used as decorations on the text pages are the work of Elizabeth.

# Table of Contents

*Elizabeth shares a joke with HRH Prince Philip at an Aidis Trust reception*

If ever proof were needed that individuals are capable of making something of their lives in spite of the most adverse conditions, this story provides it. It also shows that those who set out to overcome their disabilities will always find willing helpers.

These statements may look like platitudes but in relation to the present day conventional philosophy of life they are almost heretical. We are led to believe that environment dictates behaviour, therefore nothing much can be expected of the disadvantaged. It would be difficult to imagine a greater disadvantage than having to depend on an iron-lung for survival, yet this story shows how the spirit and the will of an individual made it possible to achieve a positive and creative life. We are also led to believe that everyone has a right to be helped and supported by other people. The fact is of course, that trying to help those who take it for granted is a chore, whereas helping those who are trying to help themselves and appreciate any help they are given is a pleasure.

Quite apart from achieving very considerable success as a painter and a teacher of ballet, Elizabeth Twistington Higgins inspired the formation of the Aidis Trust to help the severely disabled and elderly. The Trust has been particularly concerned with the development of sophisticated electronic equipment and in recent years quite remarkable progress has been achieved.

If only political theorists would base their analysis of human thought and behaviour more on people like Elizabeth Twistington Higgins than on some mythical man-in-the-street it might be better for us all.

1979

# PROLOGUE

Elizabeth Twistington Higgins, MBE, is one of the most remarkable women in Britain—though this thought has never struck her. Against odds which once seemed to be insurmountable she has become a world famous artist, has won her independence from hospitalization and has even returned to the world of dance from which she had been cruelly banished by poliomyelitis at the height of her career. She has done it by her own uncompromising determination and by becoming part of the Mouth and Foot Painting Artists, a group of professional artists who, because of disability at birth, an accident or through illness, have no use of their hands, but have learned to paint by holding the brush in the mouth or with the toes. Through this unique organisation Elizabeth has earned the freedom to express herself and to prove that the human spirit can rise above the most daunting setbacks.

This book must begin on a personal note because I first met Elizabeth twenty-five years ago when she was physically at her lowest ebb. Then I was shocked at the ironic cruelty of her situation. Mechanical breathing devices kept her body functioning when—if there had been any just-ice—she should have passed naturally beyond the agonising nightmare into which her life had been unexpectedly transformed. Yet to think of it as an injustice would have suggested an anomaly within an equitable system, and suddenly coming into contact with people stricken as indiscriminately as Elizabeth made me feel that there was no more just pattern to life than in Omar Khayyam's 'chequerboard of nights and days'.

How true that impression was in Elizabeth's case we shall see in the course of this book.

In 1954, like so many young people of my generation, I was filled with wanderlust and I left my home in Poverty Bay, New Zealand, to enjoy a sabbatical year in 'the Old Country'. After a glorious summer of European exploration I sought a job in London—preferably a warm one—to see me through the rigours of the English winter. I learned that some spent-up visitors like myself became temporary orderlies at the National Hospital for Nervous Diseases in Queen Square. In return for accommodation and five pounds a week I decided I would be happy to push a polisher or do whatever menial chores would be required—it never occurred to me that I would be involved in any actual nursing.

At an interview with the surprisingly friendly matron I was asked if I had any experience in dealing with people.

'Little people,' I said, explaining I had trained as a teacher. This answer seemed to be satisfactory as I was told to report to Ward 12. Here my idea that life would consist of going up and down corridors with a polishing machine evaporated as soon as I had donned my white coat. Through some minor misunderstanding Sister assumed that I already had some hospital experience.

'Supervise Mr Brown in his bath,' she instructed. 'He's epileptic so you have to be there in case he has a fit. If he does make sure he doesn't choke on his tongue, but don't use your finger.'

Nervously, I escorted the patient to the bathroom where he soaped himself and sang lustily while I watched him as though he was a human

bomb. Racked by unexpected responsibility, I was about to pull out the plug when he did have a fit. Knowing that I should press his tongue to prevent him swallowing it, I forgot Sister's advice and used my finger instead of a spatula, and in consequence nearly had it bitten off.

Such was my introduction to the most fascinating year I have spent, helping to look after patients of all ages and all walks of life who needed the specialist treatment provided by this great hospital. Each day I encountered humour and tragedy, hope and pain, woven together like strands of a rope. And my admiration for the nursing profession rose like the quicksilver in the thermometers I popped into patients' mouths twice a day. Sometimes nurses are said to be hard-boiled, but I rarely found that. What I did find was a professional exterior which out of necessity hid inner emotion. A nurse may leave the deathbed of a patient she has looked after for months and within minutes find herself arranging flowers on someone's locker. If feelings were allowed to be unbottled the running of a ward would be impossible.

There were thirteen different nationalities represented on the staff of Ward 12. We were a mini United Nations, only we got on perfectly well together. Apart from United Kingdom nurses, our staff included an Estonian girl, a West Indian, a Maori from my country, the inevitable Australian, an Egyptian orderly, a refugee from East Berlin and so on. The one who remains most vivid in my memory is a Czechoslovakian girl called Ilona who had come to England during the Communist take-over and gained her SRN. As a child of a Jewish mother she had survived Dachau – unlike her twin brother. Three times she had

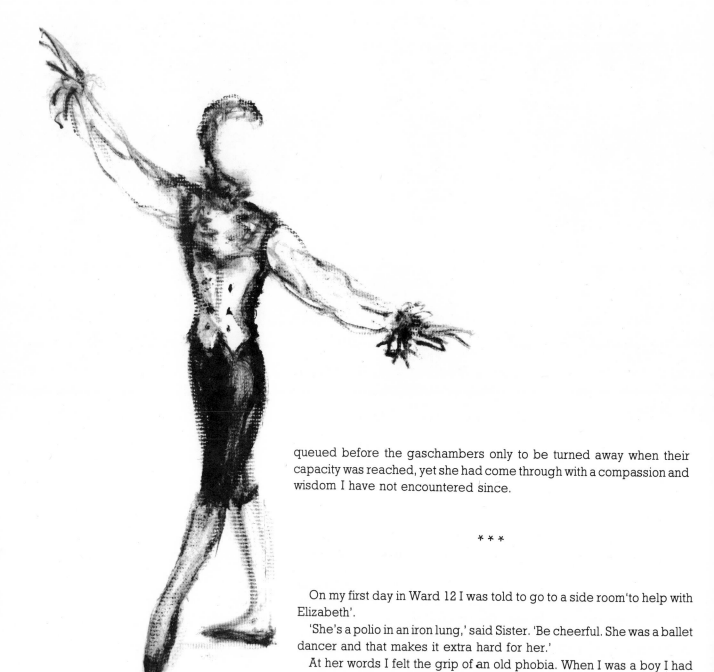

queued before the gaschambers only to be turned away when their capacity was reached, yet she had come through with a compassion and wisdom I have not encountered since.

\* \* \*

On my first day in Ward 12 I was told to go to a side room 'to help with Elizabeth'.

'She's a polio in an iron lung,' said Sister. 'Be cheerful. She was a ballet dancer and that makes it extra hard for her.'

At her words I felt the grip of an old phobia. When I was a boy I had been admitted to hospital with Potts' Disease, this undignified nomenclature meaning that I had tuberculosis of the spine. The treatment required complete immobilisation apart from my hands. I was strapped to a metal frame with weights dangling from pulleys at each end to keep me stretched out in the prone position.

My parents had been warned that I might not walk again but after a year the helmet-like arrangement holding my head was released, and the sticking plaster bandages attaching my legs to the weight cords were removed with the traditional choice of 'Slow or fast?' After I had learned to walk again I was fitted with a steel jacket which was to hold me rigid for the next four years. It had been a marvellous recovery and,

14

apart from some odd-shaped vertebrae, my only legacy of my hospitalization was a deep-seated aversion to any form of restriction.

Because I had experience of being immobilised the very thought of entombment in an iron lung filled me with horror. And now I was going to help with a patient lying helpless in one.

With trepidation I entered the room and there was the lung as horrendous as I had imagined. From a collar at one end protruded the head of a young woman. She was totally without movement from the neck down, her face was flushed because of her breathing difficulty and she was obviously very ill, yet when she saw me in the mirror placed at an angle above her face she managed to smile and say, 'Hello—you a new one?'

As I introduced myself my own selfish claustrophobic feelings melted before the impact of her predicament. She had been a successful West End dancer and ballet teacher until poliomyelitis had paralysed her within the space of two or three days. Now what hope could there be for her? As I got to know Elizabeth, through helping to lift her out of the iron lung for brief periods, or slipping into her room for a chat when work was slack, I never heard her utter a word of complaint over her lot though at times I wiped a tear from her cheek.

At Christmas that year the walking patients were sent home. We decorated the ward with paper chains, mistletoe was suspended from unlikely medical apparatus and staff members whose native tongue was not English wrote 'Merry Christmas' in their own languages with glitter on the window panes. On Christmas Day doctors did their rounds in paper hats and there were carols, but when I saw Elizabeth the contrast of this traditional jollity with her suffering struck me so deeply that I was without words.

'Never, *never,* let your face show your feelings before a patient,' Sister told me angrily when we were alone. Normally she was an understanding but efficient lady, but now she was furious with me—perhaps because her own eyes were dangerously moist.

\* \* \*

Next year I decided that England held such attraction for me that I would delay my return to New Zealand and try and get work in my chosen profession. I left the National Hospital with real regret and was lucky enough to be taken on as a reporter on Fleet Street. And the years went by with their ragbag of surprises—achievements which heralded disillusion, setbacks which turned out for the best, rare moments of joy and less rare disappointment. I became a magazine editor, then the organiser of a film festival until the time came to set forth on the perilous seas of authorship. I often wondered about Elizabeth, but apart from learning that she had left the National I did not know whether she was still being breathed artificially or whether her sufferings had come to a merciful end. Of all my patients she remained the most vivid in memory.\*

Then, almost a quarter of a century after I had left the hospital, I saw by chance Elizabeth's name in a list of television programmes. She was to appear at 11.20pm that day on a BBC *Light of Experience* production. With excitement I waited for the programme and then saw to my amazement how Elizabeth—the Elizabeth I had thought was condemned to a living death in an iron lung—had, in the words of *The Radio Times,* 'fought back to become a professional painter and founder and trainer of her own group of dancers'.

\* *Because my work entailed so much travel I had missed reading about her when she was in the news.*

Next day I sent her a letter of congratulation care of the BBC and, after receiving a friendly reply, I visited her at her home in Chelmsford. In a light and spacious room she was sitting upright in her wheelchair, her hands folded on a lace-edged cushion.

At that meeting several things impressed me. Firstly, she seemed hardly to have aged. Despite all that she had been through she was unlined and there was not a grey thread in her hair. Secondly, I was struck by the care that she obviously made sure was taken with her appearance. Her blouse was so fresh and tasteful, her fingernails were well-manicured and varnished, and her hair was just so — in fact, I found myself looking at a very attractive lady. Thirdly, within minutes, I had become so unaware she was disabled that I only just restrained myself in time from offering her a plate of biscuits when her helper brought me afternoon tea. There is that magical quality about Elizabeth which makes you completely forget illness, and if any reader fears that this book is going to be a saga of the sickbed be reassured, it is more of a unique adventure story.

But the fact was that Elizabeth was still as paralysed as when I first knew her though now she could leave the iron lung during the daytime, having mastered the extraordinary technique of breathing with her neck muscles.

After I had seen her paintings and heard more of her ballet work, it was inevitable that the question of this book should be discussed.

She finally agreed to the idea, saying 'Promise me you will write a straightforward account with no *slush!*

I promised and so the reader will find no glowing tribute to Elizabeth's fortitude, nor such phrases as 'exemplary heroism' or 'unfettered spirit' — not even such workaday adjectives as 'courageous'.

'Before you start I'd like you to see my dancers in action,' she added.

Some time later I visited the village of Therfield to see The Chelmsford Dancers perform a liturgical ballet in St Mary's Church. Having seen the *Light of Experience* programme I had some idea of what to expect, but the sheer grace of the figures moving to the music of Vivaldi and Elgar before the altar filled me with a rare sense of elation which I felt was shared by the rest of the congregation. It is no exaggeration to say that beauty was being woven out of movement before our eyes.

At one stage I glanced at the enigmatic figure in the wheelchair, and in a moment of clarity I saw that, although Elizabeth has been paralysed for nearly half her lifetime, for her the dance goes on.


West Hill Court,                                          Marc Alexander
Ratton Road,
Eastbourne.

*Elizabeth performing the* 'Legend of the Dance' *in the Solo Seal examination for the Royal Academy of Dancing in 1945*

# LES SYLPHIDES

Sadler's Wells' auditorium was charged with the electric anticipation of its audience and—as it was 1935—the fashionable tang of Turkish tobacco. From the orchestra pit squeaks and reverberations accompanied the entrance of a girl in her navy-blue best on the arm of her elder brother, and as she gazed over her programme held in white, grown-up gloves her expression did nothing to conceal the fact that this was her first night at the ballet.

Suddenly she felt engulfed as a wave of applause greeted the great Constant Lambert, the house lights dimmed to embers and the curtain rustled up on a scene which appeared to be bathed in pure moonlight.

*Les Sylphides!*

Dancers in white floated across the stage to the achingly beautiful music of Chopin, appearing to Elizabeth like beings from a world of romantic fantasy. Caught in the spell of the *ballet blanc,* something almost mystical was happening to her fourteen-year-old heart. When the curtain finally descended upon the dream she knew that all she wanted was to share its sublimity by becoming a dancer herself.

'I was so taken by *Les Sylphides,'* said Elizabeth, speaking of the experience over thirty years later. 'I think it's an exquisite ballet—pure ballet!—it's what you expect ballet to be... white dresses, beautiful music and lovely movements. It appealed to the very depths of my being, it touched a hidden chord which was probably in there all the

19

time. I think in a way it went right through to my soul. It's like listening to something superbly beautiful, you are lifted right out of yourself. It's awful coming back to earth having experienced it.'

It is not unusual for a young teenage girl to be enraptured by her first ballet and to dream of becoming another Anna Pavlova, only to forget it with the advent of the next experience in the growing-up process. But Elizabeth was not infatuated with the thought of dancing — she was truly in love with it, though soon she was to find there were plenty of problems to put her new found ambition to the test. For one thing she should have started serious training years earlier; for another she was the wrong physical shape, being too plump and too tall. Above all there was the disapproval which her father felt at the idea of his daughter dreaming of a stage career — it would have been so much easier if she could have gone to him and said, 'Daddy, I want to be a doctor.' But the sight of blood or deformity made her sick despite a background which, ironically as it was to prove, was almost completely medical.

It was because of this medical background that Elizabeth's parents met and married. The son of an Anglican clergyman in Cheshire, young Thomas Twistington Higgins became a Fellow of the Royal College of Surgeons at what today would seem an amazingly young age, and it was only natural that such a promising young man should serve King and Country in the RAMC during the First World War. After operating in the horrific conditions of forward tent hospitals, he developed a septic thumb, a terrible risk for a surgeon in those pre-penicillin days.

Because of this infection he found himself in Calais joining a stream of khaki flowing on to a troop transport soon to bear its cargo of weary and shattered humanity back to Blighty. He had been told that there would be several women on the ship, all Queen Alexandra's Nursing Sisters, and as he would be the only doctor aboard he was asked to keep an eye on them.

Before long the ship was being buffeted by the cold grey waves which had rolled down from the North Sea, and the young surgeon was called to a cabin where one of the nurses was in the throes of sea sickness. As he tended her, Tom learned that Sister Jessie Ingram had been granted compassionate leave because her father was seriously ill. He also learned that her two brothers were doctors and perhaps it was professional camaraderie which first quickened his interest in her. Having done what he could to relieve the sea sickness, he exacted her promise to meet him on *terra firma*. Presently a love affair blossomed between them but Thomas seemed reluctant to propose. He knew that soon he would be back at the Front with all its dangers, and when the war came to an end he would have no practice to return to; in fact he would not even receive a gratuity for his services. Yet he could not deny that he loved Jessie so he turned to his best friend for advice.

'Would you follow her around the town in your night-shirt?' demanded his friend.

'Well, yes, I think I would...'

'That's your answer, marry her.'

And in 1917 he did.

Soon they were sent back to their units, and it was to become a traditional tale in the family how Mother was posted ten miles 'up the line' and Father ten miles 'down the line.' When their free time coincided each walked a total of twenty miles so they could spend a few hours together.

Their first child Ian was born in 1918, soon after Tom had set up in London with only his personal determination to back him. A friend sent him his first patient — coincidentally a septic hand — and he made such a neat surgical job of it that the word spread and he never looked back.

*Thomas and Jessie*

Today Thomas Twistington Higgins is remembered as a pioneer in children's surgery, specializing in genitourology. For forty years he was to work at the Great Ormond Street Hospital for Sick Children, the last twelve of them as senior surgeon. Until the introduction of the National Health Service he gave his time free at Great Ormond Street, making his living from his private practice. He strongly disapproved of the new health service, feeling it was a privilege to be an honorary surgeon and that it was wrong to take money for doing what he regarded as his vocation — an attitude which would be regarded as archaic today.

The next child, Janet, was born to Tom and Jessie in 1920, and on Guy Fawkes Night, 1923, their second daughter Elizabeth came into the world. At that time the family was living in a terraced house overlooking Primrose Hill, London but Elizabeth's first recollections are of a large house in Well Walk, Hampstead, with a walled garden in which she romped with her brother and sister. Her father's practice must have increased because by 1929 Elizabeth remembers moving to No 34, Harley Street, and by now the family had grown with the addition of two more children and a Nanny who was to remain with the family for eighteen years. One of her nursery tales was how jealous Elizabeth tried to bite the toe of her baby brother Robin. By 1930 the family was completed by the arrival of Elizabeth's youngest sister Alison.

Inevitably one looks back through the kaleidoscope of childish

*Elizabeth had a weight problem in 1924*

*The young Elizabeth*

memories and impressions for an early hint of exceptional talent. Elizabeth and her sister Janet started at the Francis Holland School where Elizabeth experienced one of the early terrors of childhood, the fear that in the afternoon Nanny would forget to collect her and she would have to remain there for ever. The next ordeal came on Friday afternoons when she had to take part in a dancing class under the instruction of a fierce lady whom Elizabeth still remembers as 'all legs and gym slip'. However, she must have had some appreciation of Elizabeth's potential ability because she suggested to her parents that the little girl should train as a dancer, a suggestion which filled Elizabeth with such misgiving she burst into tears. Her parents' attitude was equally disapproving and the idea was rejected.

Continuing change has become such a background to our lives that today Elizabeth's middle-class childhood seems like something from a lost and strangely innocent age. Then the lamplighter and the muffin man were familiar figures; straw was spread across the street in front of houses visited by illness to muffle the sound, and children, though well loved, were continuously being told not to do things by adults who 'knew best'.

The children were frequently admonished not to stare. Nanny would say 'It's rude. Don't look now, dears, there's a poor little cripple coming. In Elizabeth's home the wireless was forbidden to the children, as was the cinema in case infection was brought home to the 'little ones'. She was a highly sensitive and volatile child — on one hand she was both determined and imaginative while on the other she was prey to fears and anxieties, but it was the subject of dress which affected her most deeply. Today she still mentally winces at the thought of those 'ghastly clothes'.

'There were horrible "reach me downs" from my eldest sister who was tall and elegant while I was fat and dumpy,' she says. 'And how I loathed liberty bodices, "chill-proof combs" and sleeping suits with back flaps. Later at school I wore a gym slip with chocolate brown stockings and navy bloomers (with a pocket for a hankie) which always sank below my knees. A friend of Ma's made us "general size" party dresses in top quality materials but — alas — in 1920's style with low waists, ribbon rosettes and frills of pink chiffon with arty sprays of flowers. Only my sister Alison had the courage to refuse to wear these. Once she was forced to go to a school party in one and she spent the whole time hidden in the cloakroom. So it was a joy to get into something made to fit by Madame Tremaine, a dressmaker, who always produced a box of chocolates after the fitting. Debenham's sales were great, too. Always beautiful quality material but unfortunately the clothes were often a size too large "because you're growing so fast".'

'I was terribly self-conscious about my appearance and I got a feeling of inferiority at being out of fashion. Was it a desire to feel inconspicuous, to be similar to everyone else? Anyhow, it was quite a barrier to overcome.'

But if young Elizabeth was embarrassed by her clothing, there were the compensations of a secure family circle in which her parents gave their children a most precious gift — their free time. There were long Sunday walks and enjoyable excursions to museums and art galleries. At Christmas time there were family charades and plays, a pantomime followed by tea at Buzzards, and an occasional visit to suitable theatrical performances — *Hiawatha* affected Elizabeth so much that she had to be removed while *The Yeomen of the Guard* made her cry for hours.

And then there were the delightfully long summer holidays in Kingsgate with tennis and croquet parties in the garden and competitions, swimming and games on the beach at Joss Bay.

But in September came the dreaded return to school and Elizabeth's

*Family group — Tom and Jessie with Nanny Gunnell, and Ian, Janet, Elizabeth and Robin.*

'Monday nerves' caused by an irrational fear of getting into trouble and the feeling that she had no ability except at needlework.

At the beginning of the nineteen-thirties Elizabeth went to the Junior St Paul's Girls' School which she enjoyed because it was new with spotless and efficient equipment. One of her happiest memories is of a singing lesson by Gustav Holst, then the musical director of the senior school. He took a dozen junior pupils and one of Elizabeth's precious childhood recollections is of this shy man gazing excitedly at the class through pebble lenses as he willed the little girls on to greater efforts.

Another aspect of school life which shed absolutely no light on Elizabeth's future was the art class — as a special dispensation she was allowed to sew instead of paint.

At Christmas time, when her father took members of the family round Great Ormond Street for the usual festivities, wards decorated with paper chains and doctors and nurses in funny hats awoke no answering chord in Elizabeth. She miserably trailed after her parents, dismayed at the sight of illness and deformity — an aversion which has remained with her all her life. She had an absolute phobia about illness and would do anything she could to avoid coming into contact with it.

The only hint as to the path which her life was to take before adolescence was that, in the security of her home, she loved to organise entertainments which included poetry, singing and dancing by herself. She also enjoyed bossing her brothers and sisters in these home productions, all costumed in bits and pieces from Nanny's ragbag.

In 1935 the family moved to a house in Highgate which had the great social advantage of a hard tennis court. This greatly appealed to Elizabeth who had previously won the North Foreland Club Junior Tournament. One of the frequent visitors was the Reverend Tubby Clayton of Toc H fame. This organisation for Christian fellowship was founded in 1915 at Poperinghe by Tubby and the Reverend Neville Talbot. The centre there was named in memory of Gilbert Talbot who

*Pas de Deux with Brighid and Elizabeth*

was killed in action in July of that year. Toc H was the army signallers' name for Talbot with H for House which, dedicated to the rest and recreation of troops, had the sign above its door 'Abandon rank ye who enter here'.

Elizabeth's parents had got to know Tubby Clayton during the war and now he and Tom sometimes took holidays together, enthusiastically visiting Iona and the Orkneys. The children were always delighted to see Tubby because of the great fund of stories which he never tired of telling them, and as Elizabeth listened to them she could have had no idea of the significance Toc H was to have later on in her life.

It was soon after the move to Highgate that Elizabeth's brother Ian, now a medical student at the London Hospital, took her to Sadler's Wells one night — and her ambition was born.

\* \* \*

When Elizabeth announced that she wanted to make the stage her career her father insisted that before any decision was reached she should take her School Certificate. To a young girl, intoxicated by *Les Sylphides,* his response must have seemed so sensible that it was unbearable. How many other teenagers have felt the same way when parents respond to their wild enthusiasms with 'adult' common sense. She passed the examination in 1939, but he was not satisfied with the result and insisted she should get her matric.

The Second World War broke out during the summer holidays which followed the examination, and when the family returned from vacation, the girls found that their school had been evacuated. To Elizabeth's delight the only school left open in Highgate was a dancing academy, and with her sisters Brighid and Alison she was enrolled there. Each day two hours of dancing lessons, which began at 8.30, were followed by general education and, helped by the fact that the wartime class she was in was made up of only five pupils, Elizabeth matriculated by Christmas.

During those hours of dancing each morning Elizabeth was taught the rudiments of Greek dancing and the Cecchetti method of ballet. With this work she began to realise the tremendous effort which a dancer must go through — the hours and hours of agonising exercise — to achieve a graceful movement.

Speaking about the Elizabeth of those days, one of her sisters said on a BBC radio broadcast: 'I can always see her in her very full skirt and black bolero, spinning round the stage and always very happy — always enjoying it and always going all out to get the thing right. She had dark hair and a round face — she was always very graceful, and she had lovely arm movements. I remember she was very fussy about her hands, and as a child she would play with them to be sure that they were in the right position and look at them in the mirror to be sure that they looked as she would like them to look. It was her arm movements I think in her dancing — and her head movements — that really made her dance as well as she did.'

Elizabeth's first taste of dancing before an audience came when the school presented a display at a garden party in aid of the Spitfire Fund. It was hardly a spectacular debut but to be in a costume, to actually perform in front of people and hear their polite applause when the group made its final curtsey, reinforced her determination to become a dancer.

She had dutifully followed her father's wishes by passing the exams he had wanted her to. Now the decision would have to be made.

While most people were occupied with what was to become known as the Phoney War, Elizabeth prepared herself for what she prayed would be her career. At the top of the house there was an empty attic where she exercised and practised several hours a day, spending the rest of her free time in reading everything she could obtain on ballet.

And then the war was phoney no more. Bombs rained on London. The old home in Harley Street was reduced to rubble and all its occupants killed. Elizabeth's father sold up at Highgate and sent his wife and children to a house in North Wales where Elizabeth continued her daily exercises at the barre. That Christmas he had leave from the Emergency Medical Centre he was in charge of to join the family. To date his only casualty had been a man whose nose had been broken when his tin hat fell on it while he was being carried on a stretcher during a Civil Defence exercise. The tradition of a family Christmas entertainment was kept up and the children, no doubt inspired by Elizabeth's enthusiasm, took the opportunity of producing a ballet.

Writing about it later, Elizabeth said, 'Robin's choreography was ingenious and included some remarkable "lifts". There was no story but plenty of movement. Three "celestial bodies", their heavenly brilliance portrayed in head-dresses made from metal milk bottle tops, encircled the "Earth" adorned with ivy leaves and fir cones. We had no music whatever so it was a purely rhythmical performance, and our parents were delighted and most impressed.'

Elizabeth may have thought that her parents were 'delighted' but it raised the old question over which there had been so many arguments. Once again she declared that it was her ambition to be a professional ballet dancer, and once again she expected to hear her father's reasoned arguments against it but, realising that she was adamant, he merely said with characteristic philosophy: 'Well, if you insist on this crazy notion, you simply must get the best possible training. Which is the top ballet school?'

'Sadler's Wells,' replied Elizabeth, unable to trust her ears.

'Right, if it's got to be, go there!'

As soon as the family returned to a house in Northwood, Elizabeth wrote to Sadler's Wells for an audition and her joy was mixed with apprehension when she received a reply telling her when to report. Soon she would have her moment of truth.

# PENNY BALLERINA

The dressing-room at the Sadler's Wells school was one of the few rooms in the building which had not needed to have its windows boarded up after bomb blast. Here a nervous Elizabeth changed into the uniform of her previous dancing-class, a white tunic tied at the waist with a crimson cord. In contrast to this childish costume the other students — all so confident and familiar with each other — wore professional black tights and tunics, and the outsider's dismay was reflected on her face.

It was obvious to Ursula Morton, the principal of the school, that Elizabeth had done hardly any proper ballet. She was having difficulty in keeping up with the class, a class which contained such students as Beryl Grey, Bunty Kelly and Lorna Mossford, and other students who were later to reach stardom. Elizabeth's own realisation of her lack of experience and poor performance, in such contrast with her ambition to become a professional dancer, brought tears to her eyes. Her distress may have touched Ursula's heart, but there is very little sentimentality in the ballet world, and it was certainly not because she felt sorry for the girl that she told her to wait after the class — behind the awkwardness she sensed a rare determination.

'Elizabeth, you've obviously got a good brain,' she told her. 'Come for a trial three-month period and then we'll talk about it again.'

These words helped to restore her deflated morale and it was with new hope that Elizabeth went to the dressing-room where one of the girls gave her advice about getting a correct outfit. Because of wartime rationing she had to make her own tunic out of a length of black silk she found in a drawer at home. And there was a pair of old cotton tights in a trunk left over from the days of dressing up for Christmas fun. Wearing these she felt more at ease when she went to Islington for her next class.

From then on it was sheer hard slogging as Elizabeth tried to make up for the years when she should have been training. When not attending Sadler's Wells she practised in the garden and before long her technique improved and her body became more supple with the endless exercises. The days she went to the ballet school were pure delight. Here classical ballet classes were taken either by Ursula Morton or Nicholas Sergueff who had formerly been regisseur at the Maryinsky Theatre in Leningrad. He had a habit of tapping the rhythm on the barre with a cane, and sometimes hit his pupils by mistake. The curriculum included a repertoire class in which the students learned excerpts from the great classical ballets. Elizabeth adored these lessons and still delights in memories of dancing as Odile or Aurora, or as a sylph. At last she was one of those fantastical elemental spirits of the air which had first kindled her enthusiasm. She found that her natural aptitude was for National or Character dancing — perhaps because it was best suited for her physique — and she had a special love for the subtle rhythm of the Mazurka which Ursula Morton patiently instilled into her pupils. But as so often seems to happen in life, this happy time was merely a prelude to disappointment.

When the probationary period was up Miss Morton asked Mrs Twistington Higgins to bring her daughter for an interview. As kindly as she could she explained that Elizabeth was physically unsuited to become a member of the Sadler's Wells Company.

Listening to these dreadful words Elizabeth felt her heart breaking, yet even at this point it did not occur to her to give up. Perhaps in some subconscious area of her personality the music of *Les Sylphides* swelled rather than faded and, as she later explained, 'I would not accept my physical limitations. I had set my heart on the stage and still felt that, by working hard, my ambition could be achieved.'

From there on the refusal to accept physical limitations has been the keynote of Elizabeth's life, though as she sat in Ursula Morton's office the limitations were those of a healthy young person not cast exactly in the mould required by Sadler's Wells. They bore no relation to the then unthinkable limitations destined to test her determination in the future.

Through the feeling of shock caused by the principal's words she heard her voice continue, suggesting to Mrs Twistington Higgins that her daughter should take her dancing exams at the Arts Educational School as in those days Sadler's Wells only trained dancers for the Company. The girl's acute disappointment was slightly lessened when it was agreed that she should continue at the Wells twice weekly.

So Elizabeth persevered, trying harder than ever to achieve her goal. She says, 'Above all I wanted to go on the stage. I'd quite made up my mind even though Miss Morton had said I was physically unsuited for the Company, which of course I obviously was. I was on the tall side, being 5'3" to 5'4", but also I had a weight problem. Really I was too big and staminawise I could never have stuck it. . .'

The school which Ursula Morton recommended was run by the famous Cone Sisters, Gracie, Lillie and Valerie, and here to Elizabeth's disgust she had to study all types of dancing which included ballroom, tap dancing and musical comedy. Modern dancing was in complete contrast to the classical ballet to which she had given her heart, and this caused her to adopt an aloof attitude to her fellow students, a psychological defence against the inferiority complex which their 'with it' attitudes tended to give her. One of the Cone's Sisters' amusing eccentricities was their strict observance of stage superstition. When Elizabeth broke a mirror she and some of her fellow pupils were sent to a nearby churchyard to bury the shards in its hallowed soil as an antidote to the evil fortune which was bound to follow such an accident.

At the end of her first term with the Cone Sisters she took her elementary examination for the Royal Academy of Dancing and, despite difficulty in hearing the examiner's commands in French, she managed to scrape through. Just over twelve months later she got her Intermediate certificate and then her Advanced Ballet in the same year — 1943. In return for giving lessons at the Cone's school, she received further training and amazingly she won the highly prized Solo Seal in 1945. This is the most difficult executant examination of the Royal Academy of Dancing and is achieved by only two or three candidates each year. At present out of a world membership of eleven thousand less than a hundred have the Seal attached to their Advanced Certificate.

Although Elizabeth now became a full-time dancing teacher at the Cone's, she still longed to perform on the stage, and this desire was heightened when she took part as a member of the *corps de ballet* with soloists from Sadler's Wells in R.A.D. Production Club performances.

Perhaps it was *Les Sylphides* again which finally decided her. She produced this ballet for the school's junior ballet group, and as one of the members could not appear for the full-scale production Elizabeth had to dance in it herself, and after this she make up her mind that she was going to try again to go on the stage. In her autobiography *Still Life,* she justified her decision by writing, 'If I was going to be a successful teacher, it was essential for me to have some experience in the theatre and I decided to leave Cone's and go on the stage. My decision was unpopular but I think it was right. I simply had to get dancing out of my system before I settled down to teaching.'

Elizabeth approached the problem of becoming a professional stage dancer with the same hard-slogging sense of purpose with which she has approached the other problems in her life. She took lessons from the most competent teachers she could find — Stanislas Idzikovski, Lydia Kyasht, Anna Sevenskaya, Lydia Sokolova and Vera Volkova at the famous West Street Dancing Studios which sadly are no longer in existence. And following the slog, an almost fairy tale element enters the story.

At the conclusion of one of Anna Sevenskaya's classes, the famous teacher told some of her pupils that there was to be an audition for a *corps de ballet* member in the musical *Song of Norway* at the Palace Theatre. It was based on the music and life of Greig, and had been choreographed by Robert Helpmann and Pauline Grant.

With a dozen other hopefuls Elizabeth presented herself before the ballet master and Moyra Fraser, the leading dancer, who were conducting the audition. Fate played into her hand that day. The ballet master was a bit uncertain about the procedure and Miss Fraser had come to help. She explained that there was a lot of character and national dancing in the show and therefore would the candidates demonstrate the Mazurka. How Elizabeth must have blessed Ursula Morton who had taught her this difficult dance so thoroughly. The result was that she was offered a contract at the wage of £6 10s a week, and

**PALACE THEATRE**

SHAFTESBURY AVENUE          LONDON, W.1
Under the Management of Tom Arnold and Emile Littler
General Manager: Francis H. Short

BOX OFFICE OPEN 10—7.30          Telephone: GERrard 6834-5

EMILE LITTLER'S

**SONG OF NORWAY**

*Presented by arrangement with Chappell & Co., Ltd.*

AN OPERETTA BASED ON THE LIFE AND MUSIC OF
**EDVARD GRIEG**

The choreography of the Concerto Ballet and Freddy and His Fiddle are by ROBERT HELPMANN. All other ballets, including the Pillow Dance and the Peer Gynt Ballet are by PAULINE GRANT.

SYMPHONY ORCHESTRA CONDUCTED BY GIDEON FAGAN

**THE OPERETTA DIRECTED by CHARLES HICKMAN**

An additional service is available to patrons of the Palace Theatre by the installation of a Cold Buffet in the Stalls Bar. Light and attractive cold savouries can be obtained prior to performances and during the interval. Patrons of the Dress Circle requiring snacks should proceed to the Stalls Bar.

thinking that Twistington Higgins was hardly suitable as a ballet name, she took the stage name of Elizabeth Scott though to her colleagues she was always Twizzy — sometimes Dizzy Twizzy.

As one would imagine, lack of rehearsal time made her first night an ordeal, especially as the production had been running for several months and Elizabeth had to fit in with a seasoned *corps de ballet* after only one morning's rehearsal. The rest of the cast were helpful to the newcomer, and the only hitch came when she made a late entry for the final ballet and nearly knocked into 'The Spirit of Norway' in the form of Moyra Fraser. Naturally she apologised after the performance and though Miss Fraser did everything she could to reassure her, for months Elizabeth always felt nervous tension grip her at that point in the performance.

* * *

Thus Elizabeth Twistington Higgins, who had begun training far too late and who did not have the right sort of body, metamorphosed into Elizabeth Scott, a professional dancer whose time was taken up by eight performances a week plus rehearsals and the dancing classes which she continued to attend. After a few months she joined two fellow artistes from the show to give Sunday ballet performances at Butlin's Holiday Camps, and again her sparkling rendition of the Mazurka proved to be a popular asset.

After Christmas she successfully auditioned for the new Ivor Novello musical *King's Rhapsody*. The book and play were by Christopher Hassall and the choreography by Pauline Grant. The show's extravagant colour and costumes delighted Elizabeth; the dress she wore for the ballroom scene — a delicate creation in pink and grey trimmed with silver and white — cost two hundred pounds.

In contrast with post-war austenty *King's Rhapsody* was like an explosion of gaiety and warmth. The production opened in Manchester, and after three weeks came to the Palace Theatre in London where it was an instant success. Elizabeth was to remain with the cast during its long run and her most lasting impression of the show is the happy atmosphere generated by Ivor Novello himself. The young dancer found him to be kindly to all who worked with him. Often he arranged outings for the members of the company or invited them to parties at his own home. At first Elizabeth was amazed at the beautiful antiques and original paintings it contained, and the fact that his famous jade collection was scattered about the house and not even locked away during the huge anniversary celebrations which he loved to hold.

On two occasions during *King's Rhapsody* the theatre closed for a week, and on each occasion the staff was given a holiday partly at Ivor's expense. Typically Elizabeth — forever a perfectionist — spent the first such holiday in Paris where she attended ballet classes given by Olga Preobrajenskaya.

Elizabeth has many treasured memories of Ivor Novello but the most revealing was when her brother had to undergo an operation. The war had been over for several years and now it is hard to believe that Government-imposed food rationing still had a couple of years to run until it was abolished in 1953. In London fresh eggs were hard to come by yet each week Ivor sent new laid eggs to Elizabeth's dressing-room

*Elizabeth in* 'Song of Norway'

*The ballroom scene in 'King's Rhapsody'*

for the patient.

One would have thought that with doing eight shows a week Elizabeth's enthusiasm for dancing would have been satisfied, but one of her characteristics is that she attempts to stretch time by the concentration of work. Although still enjoying *King's Rhapsody,* she was vaguely discontented. As she later explained, 'I felt that being on stage wasn't really doing much good for anybody other than myself—so I thought that I'd like to do something for other people, although I didn't know what. I like children very much, so I enquired about nursery school activities and was put in touch with the Froebel Foundation. It just so happened that the management committee of Coram's Fields were planning to start some pre-school activities to give the local mothers a bit of a rest from their children. So I started a dancing class twice weekly, and each session cost them three old pence.' She taught in the old band room in which Handel had rehearsed his famous Foundling choir.

The site of Coram's Fields in Bloomsbury was just a few hundred yards away from Great Ormond Street Hospital. The centre took its name from Captain Thomas Coram. Born in Lyme Regis in 1668, he started life as a shipwright and then went to Taunton, Massachusetts, later living in London after being shipwrecked off Cuxhaven in 1719. Here he worked at his plan for a foundling hospital in Bloomsbury, and in 1743 it was

*Elizabeth with her little pupils in Coram's Fields pre-school activities in 1950*

opened for the reception of five hundred children. He spent so much of his own resources of energy and cash pursuing his objective that he fell into poverty soon after the inauguration of his home, until his friends rallied round and raised an annuity of £161 for him.

In 1926 a proposal that the Covent Garden Market should be removed to the ten-acre Coram's Fields met such a storm of protest that the scheme had to be abandoned, and the site was secured thanks to money supplied by Lord Rothermere, the London County Council and local borough councils so that it was laid out as a children's playground and opened in 1936.

When Elizabeth began her pre-school dancing group another Coram's Fields' experiment was the Penny Concerts which, as the name suggests, were monthly concerts held on Saturday mornings where children were admitted for a penny to be entertained by musicians from the Royal Academy of Music. Violet Graham, of the Academy, had been running the scheme for twelve months when Elizabeth joined it to present dancing items, which she did for the next four years.

Soon her activities went beyond her pre-school dancing class and the Penny Concerts. In one corner of Coram's Playing Fields there was an open-air school for delicate children with chest and respiratory complaints — in retrospect another touch of irony.

'They had a very enlightened headmistress who thought it would be a good thing if I ran a music and movement class for them, too,' recalls Elizabeth. 'She gave the LCC no peace until she had persuaded them to let me join her staff as a visiting teacher for two mornings a week.'

Prior to the school's birthday word spread that Elizabeth was organising a special celebration performance in which her friends from *King's Rhapsody* would take part, having rehearsed for it backstage and and on the roof of the Palace Theatre. Costumes had been a problem until Ivor Novello heard about Elizabeth's spare-time activity and persuaded a theatrical costumier to provide them free.

So many hundreds of eager children turned up at Coram's Fields that

*'The Doll that came to Life', with Mavis Trail as the doll and Elizabeth as the child, at the 1951 Christmas Penny Concert*

the police had to be called in to control the crowd, but the performance was a joyous success and Elizabeth earned the nickname of 'The Penny Ballerina'.

It is hard to see how she coped so successfully with her full-time dancing in the theatre and her work with different groups of children. For example on Wednesdays and Saturdays before she turned up for the matinees of *King's Rhapsody* she had already taken three morning classes at Coram's Fields. Yet when it came to her beloved dancing, or the teaching of it, she could always summon up more energy or find extra time by sacrificing even more of her private life.

By 1951 Elizabeth had been on the stage for six years and this experience had done something to lessen the natural shyness which was in such contrast to the basic determination of her character, but she never completely lost the nervousness she suffered before her first entry on stage.

Then everything seemed to change.

After the final curtain call one evening Ivor Novello said goodnight to the company as usual. Next day they were stunned to hear of his death. True to theatrical tradition there was no performance that night. The show went on the following day but though *King's Rhapsody* was to continue for several months the inspiration seemed to have gone out of it.

It was during this gloomy period that Elizabeth decided the time had come for a change in the direction of her life. Her experience with the Coram's Fields classes and the Penny Concerts told her that she would find more satisfaction in teaching and when *King's Rhapsody* came to an end she did not audition for any more shows.

Her last public performance was a glittering farewell to the theatre. It was the Ivor Novello Memorial Show at the Coliseum with such stars as Noel Coward, Gracie Fields, John Gielgud, Kirsten Flagstaed and Emlyn Williams.

*Elizabeth's Italian dance at a Penny Concert*

*Arnott Mader and Elizabeth in 'Tarantella' — an open-air rehearsal*

The curtain went up on a Ruritanian scene in which girls in pink Empire-style gowns waltzed gaily with partners in extravagant blue and gold uniforms to music from Novello's most successful shows. As Elizabeth whirled on the stage what memories came crowding back with the romantic music. Despite everything, she had done what she set out to do, she had become a dancer and now, at the very height of her career, she was about to embark on what to her was a more challenging vocation. Once a challenge is overcome Elizabeth has always had to seek the next one.

When the dancers left the stage she stood chatting to an amusing man in the wings, then returned to her dancing partner who was waiting for her at the side of the stage.

'You've got a nerve, haven't you?' he said.

'What do you mean?'

'You know who you were talking to, don't you?' She shook her head and he told her — in her excitement Elizabeth did not realise that she had been joking with Noel Coward.

\* \* \*

Having changed the course of her career Elizabeth found herself busier than ever. While continuing her work at Coram's Fields she held her own dancing classes at the Art Workers' Guild Hall in Queen Square, Bloomsbury, which stood opposite the great brick bulk of the National Hospital for Nervous Diseases. These private dancing classes had started at the request of mothers of children attending Coram's Fields and it left her little time for a personal life, and although she had boy friends it was lucky—Elizabeth was to think later in life—that she had no deep emotional attachment. Dancing was still her first love, and

34

for Elizabeth the perfectionist the right man had not come into her life. But she was still a young woman, there was plenty of time left for marriage, settling down and hopefully children, but at the moment there was another class to fit in, costumes to arrange, a ballet to choreograph...

When the Great Ormond Street Hospital for Sick Children planned to celebrate its centenary she was asked to produce a ballet to entertain ex-patients in a huge marquee in the hospital's courtyard, while the young patients would view it from the balconies of the building.

Twenty of her pupils danced her *1852 Ballet*, in costumes which she had designed after hours of research in the print room of the Victoria and Albert Museum. It seemed such a pity that after so much effort it should have only one showing, so she took it to clubs for elderly people and schools for handicapped children. This led to her teaching at the Mary Ward School for the Physically Handicapped. After a performance there the headmistress explained that she was short of a kindergarten teacher and would she help until a professional teacher arrived. 'I had always had a horror of illness and disfigurement and I had to steel myself to face these pathetic little people.' Elizabeth says. 'My heart ached for them. . . The first few days were a terrible strain, but I gradually got used to it.'

In 1953 Elizabeth's father retired to a village in Kent where he planned to devote his time to writing. As a result she and her brother Robin shared a flat in the Chelsea Studios which was in effect a delightful walled village created by an Italian sculptor for London artists. Behind the high wall it was a bit of old Italy complete with sculptures, wrought iron work, gay tiles, vines and masses of climbing plants, such as laburnums, wisteria and jasmine.

Somehow Elizabeth found time to become involved in a different kind of work which gave her great satisfaction. Until dancing became her obsession, her greatest pleasure had been in needlework which later stood her in good stead when it came to making costumes for herself and her pupils' displays, darning ballet shoes, creating clothes and wedding dresses. It was Coronation Year and an exhibition of the Royal Coronation Robes was planned, to be held at St James's Palace, and knowing Elizabeth's interest in sewing, the principal teacher of the Royal School of Needlework asked her if she would like to be involved.

This exhibition opened a week after the Coronation on June 2, and Elizabeth became one of the dozen helpers who worked six-hour shifts under the watchful eyes of the C.I.D.

'The opening night was televised, with a commentary by Richard Dimbleby,' Elizabeth wrote later. 'It was opened by Queen Elizabeth the Queen Mother, accompanied by the Duke and Duchess of Gloucester and the Princess Royal. It was very colourful and the Queen Mother was wearing a tiara and shimmering crinoline. She looked superb, and I was thrilled and delighted when she shook my hand. My days seemed very hectic, rushing between teaching, the Palace, the flat, always on the go.'

But Elizabeth was not to be on the go for much longer. Three weeks after the exhibition opened she was struck down by the cruellest blow fate could mete out to a ballet dancer.

*Elizabeth with puppy, 1952*

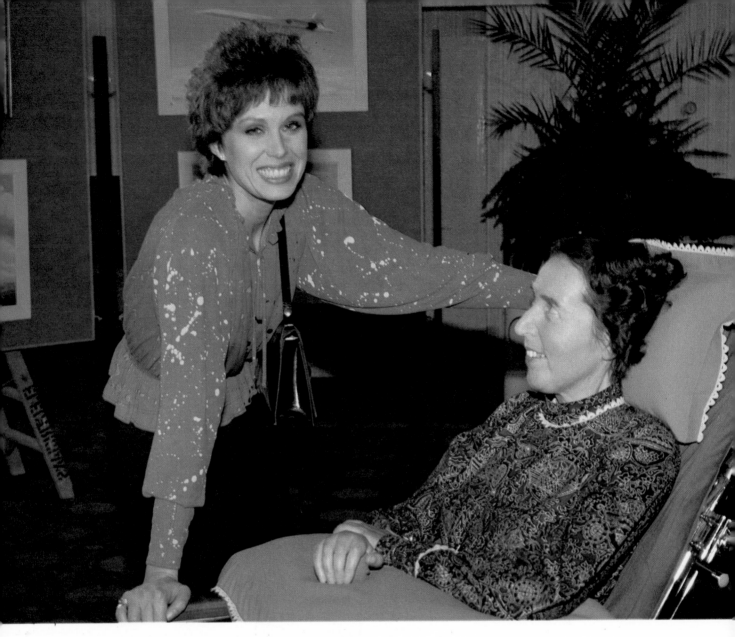

*Joanna Lumley with Elizabeth at an exhibition of the work of Mouth and Foot painters at Allders or Croydon. (Photographed by Marc Alexander.)*

# DREAM AND NIGHTMARE

Elizabeth was dancing down London's Wigmore Street to the sound of wonderful music. Pedestrians stared while she whirled gracefully between them on the pavement, and the faces of many broke into spontaneous smiles as her unexpected appearance brought a touch of beauty to their humdrum day. In a succession of shop windows the girl saw her reflection, the vivid colours of her ballet costume giving brief, exotic touch to the merchandise behind the glass. On and on she danced, and as the crowds began to applaud she felt she could dance forever. Never had she enjoyed such a sense of freedom...

As she opened her eyes there was the thunder of applause in her ears, but it was not for her street performance — it was from a radio which had just presented music from a Promenade Concert. And like a sinister obligato came a regular swishing sound which told her that she was once more in the waking nightmare which had gone on since she had been rushed into an iron lung. It was hard for her to believe that only a few days ago she had been dancing just as actively as she had in the dream — now her life depended on the machine in which in which she lay.

In July, 1953, Elizabeth's three-month-old nephew Johnny was admitted to the Great Ormond Street Hospital for Sick Children with suspected meningitis. Her sister Janet telephoned the alarming news and, as she was breast feeding the baby, added that she was going to stay with him in the hospital where she had been a ward sister before her marriage, and where her husband Dave was a physician. Could

The '1852 Ballet', performed at Great Ormond Street Hospital in 1952

Elizabeth look after their other child Nicholas, then eighteen months old?

The baby's condition worsened and one evening Janet returned to the flat not expecting him to live through the night. But at Great Ormond Street, the fight for his life continued, everyone giving of their very best for the tiny patient. Miraculously John survived, but a week later Janet was taken ill with the same mysterious symptoms. She was admitted to the National Hospital in Queen Square which is just round the corner from Great Ormond Street.

Meanwhile Elizabeth found Nicholas very fretful despite all the comforting cuddles she could give him. She came to the conclusion that he was missing his mother, and only later was it realised that he too was sick.

The following Saturday Elizabeth went to Queen Square to take her usual classes in the hall opposite the hospital where her sister was now a patient. Down the road was Coram's Fields where she had become the Penny Ballerina; nearer at hand was the Great Ormond Street Hospital to which her father had devoted most of his working life, and where her nephew was recovering from his undefined illness.

As she walked in the bright sunshine Elizabeth realised that she was not feeling her usual healthy self so she went into a chemist's shop and bought a thermometer. It registered a temperature of 102 degrees. Immediately after classes she went to the Great Ormond Street Hospital to consult her brother-in-law. Because it had never occurred to her that she could be ill she had not taken the trouble to register with a general practitioner. David's advice was to go home and if the temperature continued to let him know.

Back at the Chelsea Studios she found that her temperature had risen even higher. David visited her but apart from slight pharyngitis he was unable to diagnose the cause of the trouble.

She had planned to go to Kent to spend the weekend with her parents, so he gave her some tablets and said that if her temperature was normal in the morning it would be safe to make the journey.

When she awoke the next morning she felt better and set off to see her parents. After meeting her at the station, her father drove to the coast so that she could have a view of the sea which she found calming after the anxiety of the past fortnight. Lunch was followed by one of those golden afternoons which sometimes lift the English summer into something more beautiful than mere warm weather and clear skies. Feeling deathly tired, Elizabeth was content to laze the hours away in the garden.

The following day she still had a feeling of exhaustion and decided not to return to London. She believed it was a reaction to her worry over Johnny and Janet, and that rest in the quiet, companionable atmosphere of her parents' home would soon restore her. In the afternoon she took the dog for a walk over the fields and during it realised she was not just tired but ill. Her head hurt abominably and the back of her neck became stiff. As soon as she got home she went to bed and in the morning her father called in Dr Boulden, the local G.P., who was later to become a true friend. Her condition worried him so much that he decided to perform a lumbar puncture.

When he inserted the long needle into her back she experienced a most unusual reaction; she became aware of the whole pattern of her nervous system as though there was electricity coursing through it, rather like an electronic diagram which lights up for teaching purposes. At the same time she experienced a ghastly feeling that her hands were turning into claws.

The results of the lumbar puncture underlined the fact that there was something very wrong with her. As there were no hospital beds available locally it was decided that she should be admitted to the National Hospital to be with her sister—a decision to which Elizabeth owes her life. Her mother rode in the ambulance for the four-hour journey during which Elizabeth once again had the sensation that her hands, with which she had made such graceful movements when dancing, were becoming claw-like. Yet when they reached Bloomsbury she still managed to direct the driver to the hard-to-find entrance to Queen Square.

Another touch of irony: as Elizabeth was taken by trolley into the hospital on one side of the square, her pupils were arriving for their class on the other. She was worried lest any of them saw her being wheeled ignominiously into the towering building. Here she was taken to a ward and had the satisfaction of being put in a bed next to Janet. As yet her complaint had not been diagnosed so, in case the sisters were infectious, a curtain was kept drawn about them.

It is always an ordeal to be admitted to hospital for the first time, especially when you have no idea of what ails you, and, like so many new patients, Elizabeth lay in her bed and wondered at the strange noises and meaningless conversation which reached her through the curtain. In such a situation it is so easy to interpret a yawn as a groan or a sudden cackle of laughter as a cry of agony. One bit of conversation Elizabeth treasures took place between an unseen doctor and patient.

Silence for a moment.

'Show me your teeth.'

'They're on the locker, doctor.'

Elizabeth was subjected to various tests, none of which indicated what was the matter with her, and the cheerful way in which she co-operated with the doctors may have stopped them from appreciating fully the seriousness of her condition. On the morning after she was admitted she lost control of her left arm, and when she tried to reach a glass of water the effort so exhausted her that Janet left her bed to help her. Next day she found herself panting and yet only able to manage to inhale half-breaths. In panic she called for help and, as a nurse rushed to her, Elizabeth suddenly knew what was the matter with her.

'I've got polio, haven't I?' she cried. 'I'll never dance again!'

'You're going to be worse before you're better,' replied the nurse in a dour Scottish accent. It was at this point, Elizabeth believes, that it was first realised that she, her sister and the baby had been infected by polio.

People materialised around the bed and then it was being wheeled rapidly out of the ward. Looking back Elizabeth saw Janet staring after her with an expression of utter grief on her face.

As Elizabeth put it later, 'They whizzed me out of the ward, wheeled me along seemingly endless corridors to a room on Ward 12 where I was shoved in an iron lung, and that was that!'

*After retirement — Tom and Jessie in Kent.*

* * *

When Elizabeth was a small girl Nanny had shown her a newspaper photograph of the first iron lung. And there had been a lot of publicity when the paralysed son of an American millionaire had been taken to Lourdes in one mounted in a special vehicle. The ugly, tank-like contraption had given the child nightmares. She knew that the patient's head had to be squeezed through a cruel-looking rubber collar to make an airtight seal round the neck. But now, a score of years later, she felt immense relief when her childhood memory was exorcised by the sight of a nurse unfastening a press-stud to open the collar for her head to pass through. The motor of the lung was switched on and Elizabeth first heard its rhythmic 'swish-clonk'. As the powerful pump alternately increased and decreased the air within the tank, her lungs responded to the varying pressure and her gasping fit was over. Being able to breathe again gave her false hope. She thought that she would only need a few hours in the machine and then she would be returned to the ward. But that evening when a nurse switched off the machine, she found she could not breathe at all. She was totally paralysed.

Poliomyelitis, earlier known by the dread name of Infantile Paralysis, was one of the most feared diseases in the world. It attacks the nerve cells which control muscle movement and during the early stages the muscles which are used most tend to be the worst affected. However, it does not affect the sensory nerves so that although Elizabeth cannot move her limbs she is acutely conscious of any pain in them. Only three months after she became paralysed the polio virus was isolated and soon the famous Salk vaccine made polio epidemics a thing of the past. But while the disease has been brought under control, its effects live on in victims such as Elizabeth.

At first she did not realise the full impact of her illness because she was told, 'You've got to give it six to nine months to regain any movement that there might be in your body.'

For the first few weeks in the lung when she was very ill Elizabeth thinks that she hardly slept at all. She had hallucinations rather than dreams which seemed to be made up of 'masses of movement', and she was acutely aware of colours, mostly reds and pinks, which were

*Rudolph Nureyev holds one of Elizabeth's paintings in a film on her life made by*
*Aquarius Films and produced by David Richardson.*
(Photograph Marc Alexander.)

constantly pulsating to a rhythmical sound which must have been the noise made by the machinery of the lung.

'I used to lie in the lung and mentally do a ballet barre,' she recalls. 'You know, go through various exercises in my mind because my father had said, "When your brain messages go to a particular part of your body, if it's going to move it will move." I think this was about the most depressing thing I could have done because day after day, week after week, and — in the end — month after month, nothing happened.'

'I have only a very slight movement in my right hand which took, I suppose, three or four months to show any sign of life. It has gradually got stronger, but I think I knew within that period that the prospect wasn't very good.'

During this dreary time Elizabeth used to dream quite normally, often about dancing as in the Wigmore Street dream. Later she had a period of dreaming that she was disabled — she would find herself hobbling about in callipers, and then she would wake to find herself even more disabled than she had dreamed.

To the staff of Ward 12, where the iron lung stood in a small room overlooking Queen Square, Elizabeth's plight was so distressing that sometimes experienced nurses had to leave hurriedly so she would not notice their tears. When she was very ill several declared it would be a mercy if she did not recover — all that the future could hold for her was pain, imprisonment and frustration. And yet — although it seemed impossible at the time — they were to be proved completely wrong.

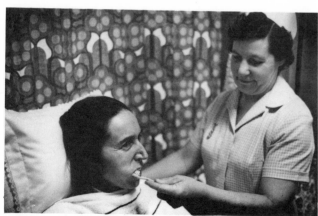

*Iris Rose cleaning teeth*

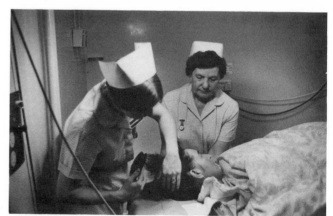

*Hair brushing*

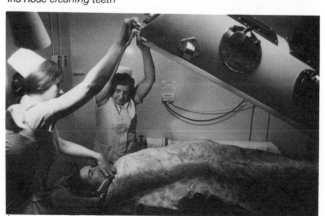

*Locking down*

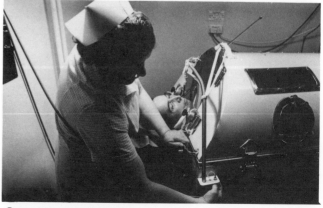

*Connecting possum lifeline*

# GUINEA PIG

Because Elizabeth was infectious everyone who entered her room at the National Hospital wore surgical masks and gowns which gave them a strange anonymity. Often she could only recognise them by their eyes.

'Lying flat on my back, night and day, with only my head outside my machine and surrounded by these masked figures, I became very concious of the beauty of people's eyes,' she was to write later. 'If the saying is true that "the eyes are the mirrors of the soul", then I was being cared for by Saints.'

By a stroke of luck the National was the one hospital in the world where a positive pressure breathing machine was being developed. The apparatus was to become known as the Beaverometer, named after its inventor Dr Beaver who was the senior anaesthetist at the hospital. The idea behind it was for a small compact machine to provide artificial respiration for a patient outside an iron lung. In the latter the patient's chest is expanded through 'negative pressure', or vacuum, so that air is drawn into the lungs; a positive pressure machine aerates the lungs by pumping air directly through a mask fitted over the patient's mouth and nose. If Elizabeth could be ventilated by this apparatus it would be possible for her to leave the lung for necessary medical attention, though so far positive pressure had only been tried on comatose patients needing life support.

Her first experience with it was terrifying. A group of masked figures materialised round her and before she was aware of what was happening, an anaesthetist's mask was clamped over her face. To her alarm the iron lung pump was turned off. Her lungs cried out for air, but how do you tell people you are suffocating when you are completely paralysed and most of your face is covered with rubber? She made a

desperate effort and managed to shake her head to indicate she could not breathe. Dr Beaver was sent for and reassured her, explaining exactly how his machine worked so that she would be able to co-operate in the use of it. After this she faced the ordeal of the new breathing equipment four times a day when she was taken from the lung.

Elizabeth had hardly ever experienced illness before she became a patient — she had been used to being in complete control of her body. As a dancer she was much more conscious of it than most people and now it had become an object kept going by medical plumbing. She felt humiliated by her helplessness and everything that it meant — especially the lack of privacy when out of the lung.

Every six hours her team would descend upon her. It consisted of an anaesthetist, a physiotherapist, two nurses and engineers who kept their ears cocked to the rhythm of the air pump. Everyone there knew they had about twenty minutes to do all that was required. During that time Elizabeth was medically examined, given enemas, catheterisation, physiotherapy and was washed. The anaesthetist remained at her head, constantly adjusting the mask without which she would collapse. On several occasions the machine broke down and, as everything darkened before her eyes, she had the feeling of dropping away from the world into oblivion. Seconds later the shaken nursing staff would have her back in the iron lung, and as the air once more filled her lungs she would return to life trembling with shock.

'These sessions were absolutely ghastly,' Elizabeth recalled later. 'For me they were public torture sessions. My limbs hurt so much when I was moved that the tears streamed down my face and I wasted energy crying out for help. I also hated the weird, remote, antiseptic atmosphere in which I was forced to live, but if I had not felt so ill and frightened, I might have enjoyed the theatrical quality of the staff's performance — it was so polished and professional. I am sure it was due to the speed and efficiency of this team that I am alive today.'

After Elizabeth had been in the iron lung for about five weeks a new Residential Medical Officer, Dr Roger Gilliat, was appointed and he became very involved in the development of the Beaverometer. His attitude to life was very serious — Elizabeth says it took three weeks to coax a smile out of him — but he had great sympathy with her situation. When he went into her room his greeting was not the stock 'And how are we today?' but 'What are your interests in life, young lady?' These few words had a very encouraging effect on the patient who felt she had lived a cabbage-like existence since she had been admitted.

Here was someone who was interested in her as a person, as well as a difficult medical case. He was quick to understand her fear of suffocation when she was removed from the lung and immediately ordered another machine to be brought in as a standby. Coupled with a double supply of oxygen by the lung, it meant that if one machine failed the other could function immediately. This reassured the patient, and her ears no longer strained to detect a change in the note of the motor, nor did her heart race in such panic if the room was filled with a sudden silence.

Yet from time to time there were still technical hitches — a lead would be lost, an oxygen cylinder would become exhausted or a tube would fall off.

'Dr Gilliat ran up several flights of stairs regularly to put things right when they went wrong,' Elizabeth says. 'Several times I nearly snuffed it. But through it all I thought, "I am pioneering a new machine — at least I am still worth something."'

It was not just the technical aspects of the case which concerned the doctor; behind his austere facade there was great sensitivity and understanding. On the day he first saw Elizabeth he made arrangements for her to be provided with a record player and an endless supply of records from a nearby library. Though this music upset Elizabeth at first, it was to provide her only escape from the tormented mental state she suffered while seeking to come to terms with the catastrophe which had overwhelmed her.

With the co-operation of Dr Beaver, Dr Gilliat set about improving the Beaverometer, and in this he was fortunate in having Elizabeth as a guinea pig who could report her reactions precisely, something which unconscious patients had obviously been unable to do. He told Elizabeth that it was his intention to make the mask of the positive pressure machine 'nurse-proof'. At that time the Beaverometer could only be used with an anaesthetist in charge of the air intake and this was its great drawback because in busy hospitals anaesthetists are not always available. The problem was overcome by replacing the mask with an aqualung mouthpiece which she used with a nose-clip. Elizabeth soon learned to keep it in her mouth and this meant that an anaesthetist was no longer required. Unfortunately its weight made it necessary for a nurse to hold it and even with this support it was inclined to make the patient's gums bleed.

Despite her own predicament Elizabeth's interest in the development of the machine approached that of her doctors, though at times Dr Gilliat's enthusiasm exhausted her. One evening he turned up at ten o'clock to test out a new version of the Beaverometer, one which was powered by compressed air as many life-support systems are today.

The night sister looked more and more anxious as the minutes, then hours, went by. She was worried because her charge had been given her usual sleeping drugs and now she was visibly wilting, but the doctor had no sense of time when work was involved. By midnight he was still making adjustments and checking the performance, while Elizabeth felt more and more ghastly.

By a quarter-to-one she could take no more, she spat the mouthpiece out and declared she would not go on. The doctor was very cross when he left the room but next morning he returned to apologise for having been carried away. He told Elizabeth that she could have an easy day as he was going to try the equipment on himself. Later on he got another doctor to operate the Beaverometer while he took the role of a patient — with the result he fainted.

'I felt I'd got my own back,' Elizabeth recalls with a smile. 'But he was obviously doing valuable research, today every intensive care unit has life support machines which all stem from the early Beaverometer. I must say that it was the Beaverometer and a splendid team of nurses, who were very quick on the draw, which kept me alive. I do feel I owe my life to Dr Beaver and that team.'

One day Dr Gilliat brought a group of visitors to see Elizabeth. They were members of the Everest Expedition which included Griff Pugh, the team's physiologist and Tom Bourdillon, who was later to die tragically in a climbing accident. They were fascinated to see the Beaverometer in operation because Tom Bourdillon had used a rather similar closed-circuit oxygen device in the Himalayas, though the problem there had been the exact opposite to that faced by Elizabeth. The mountaineers were husky men with large vital capacities but without air, in contrast Elizabeth was surrounded by air but was without breathing capacity.

Much later, when she had left her beloved National Hospital for the Royal National Orthopaedic Hospital at Stanmore, Elizabeth again became a guinea pig for a new type of breathing-machine, this time it was a portable cuirass-type respirator which was in effect a wearable iron lung. Two doctors had been developing it and it was nearing

completion when Elizabeth arrived. She found the cuirass to be made of a light plastic which fitted round her torso with a sponge rubber seal at each end to allow a partial vacuum to be created — thus expanding the chest — by an extraction pump connected by a flexible tube.

The first patient to try the cuirass had been a paralysed doctor, the second was Elizabeth. The problem she found with the cuirass was that though it came in three sizes, physiotherapists had been used as models and they are usually buxom girls, or seem so when compared to patients with paralysed chests. Elizabeth had a medium size which 'fitted where it touched' so she had to have a special Dunlopillo 'shape' made which fitted more snugly and bore the main pressure of the device. A constant problem was that these seals rubbed Elizabeth's skin, especially above the hip bones. Nevertheless, she was to use a cuirass for sleeping for fifteen years until it could no longer ventilate her properly and she had to go back into an iron lung.

* * *

During her first few months at the National Hospital Elizabeth felt that she was going to be entombed in the iron lung forever. Physiotherapists worked on her to try and restore some breathing capability and, as there was no chance of her chest muscles ever working again, they concentrated on developing her neck muscles which they hoped she would be able to use *consciously* to draw air into her lungs. Progress was so slow that she felt there was no progess at all.

At regular intervals Dr Gilliat would arrive with his stopwatch to check on any improvement. The lung would be switched off so Elizabeth had to try and breathe unaided — with the result she was blue almost immediately. After fourteen weeks she was able to last for thirty seconds; after seven months she could manage fifteen minutes on her own.

As this form of breathing improved it was decided that Elizabeth should be placed on a rocking bed — and the author remembers vividly helping to lift her on to the contraption for the first time. To the spectator the bed looked as though it had been designed to make the patient seasick. It was balanced on a fulcrum with an electric motor that made each end rise and fall like a see-saw. This motion made the patient's diaphragm drop down as her head came up, then pushed it up as her head went down.

The rocking exercise had to stop when Elizabeth developed a kidney stone — always a hazard to paralysed people — which made her very seriously ill. She became so sick that a mirror above the iron lung, used for watching television and talking to visitors through was taken away so that she would not see* how bad she looked. Somehow she survived on endless injections, intravenous drips and nasal feeding.

The crisis passed when the stone was dispersed medically — it is doubtful if Elizabeth could have survived a surgical operation at that time — and the physiotherapy sessions began again with the physiotherapist using the old fashioned 'artificial respiration' technique to develop her neck muscles. Every day the number of

*A clever technician reversed the polarity of the set so that the image appeared back-to-front on the screen and therefore the right way round in the mirror.

*Second cubicle used as a studio when available.*

breaths Elizabeth was able to inhale on her own was counted, and when the daily score was increased by one or two it was a matter for mutual congratulation.

One day there was great jubilation in Elizabeth's room, she had managed to breathe a hundred times. Her nursing team began to hope that it migh be possible for her to have relatively long spells free from any breathing apparatus. But however much she improved, Elizabeth would always have to be machine-breathed when she slept because breathing could never again be an automatic process. Every breath she has taken herself since 1953 has been the result of deliberate mental commands to her neck muscles, commands that must be given consciously no matter what else may be claiming her attention. It is a situation which almost defies the imagination of a normally healthy person whose *medulla oblongata* controls his or her breathing automatically.

Another thing that Elizabeth had to learn when in the iron lung was to speak in time with the air leaving her body.

'The specialists were surprised how easy I found it to talk in the lung,' she says. 'You can only speak as it breathes you "out", you can't speak as it breathes you "in". This is obvious if you've done any voice training — which I had done in the course of my career — but talking is a terrific effort and with the noise of the pump people can't always make out what you say.'

Elizabeth has to judge her sentences to fit in with her breathing, though very occasionally she still gets caught mid-sentence. A recent example of this demonstrates the embarrassment to which she can be subjected.

One evening she had been put in the iron lung for the night when she said to a nurse, 'Close the window. . .' She was going to add 'please' but before she could get the word out her breath began to be drawn in and she was momentarily struck dumb. She was furious when the nurse turned to her and said, 'You might at least have said please!'

\* \* \*

Once the National RMO was checking Elizabeth's progress he remarked, 'You're lucky to be here.'

'Oh yes,' she answered, 'I might have been in an isolation hospital, I suppose.'

'No, I don't mean that — you're lucky to be here at all.'

His words brought home to Elizabeth just how desperately ill she had been and the amazing progress she had made.

After two-and-a-quarter years at the National she could go for two hours outside the iron lung, though at mid-day she would be returned to it for a rest before having an afternoon spell on her own. Since then Elizabeth has improved to the point of being independent of machine breathing for the whole day which, considering how completely she is paralysed, is something of a medical miracle.

'I suppose I was lucky being in a very good physical shape before I became ill,' she comments. 'I didn't smoke, so my chest was good. I haven't had a lot of chest complications, but catching a cold is very dangerous for me because I have no cough reflex. It's very easy to drown in your own secretions, so respiratory infections are my No 1 medical hazard.'

Recently one of Elizabeth's doctors described her physical problems

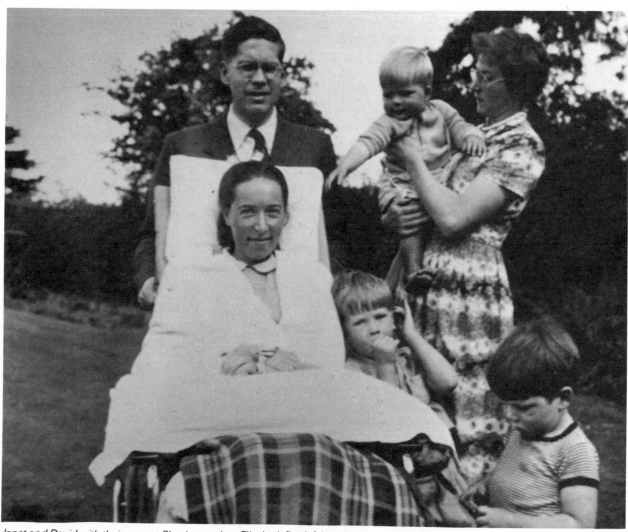

*Janet and David with their sons at Cheshunt, when Elizabeth first left hospital*

as follows: 'Her paralysis is almost complete as far as movement is concerned, but not as far as sensation is concerned. She can feel absolutely everything, so that if, for example, she feels a pain or even an itch she not only feels the irritation, but she's conscious of the fact that she cannot do a thing about it, and this must be an absolutely appalling thing for her. We do not realise how we are continuously moving. Myself, I'm a fidgity person and I could not stay still for more than a few seconds. I'm always playing with my fingers or something. For somebody to have all these desires to move and to be unable to do so must be literally hell, very much like the Chinese water torture where you are subjected to a continuous stimulus about which you can do nothing.

'As far as her limited neck movement is concerned, it's impossible to over emphasise how important this is, because, not only does her life depend upon it, her career depends upon it. Her breathing muscles — the ordinary unconscious breathing muscles that we breathe with, the ones between the ribs and diaphragm — are all completely paralysed. It is an intense physical effort for her to breathe, because she is doing a job for which Nature provides twelve ribs, twenty-four muscles between the ribs, more or less, and a very powerful muscular diaphragm. Instead of being able to use this, she has to use two very thin muscles in her neck, part of whose function she has to spare for other things as well. I remember once, when I was talking to her and something distressing occurred, she began to cry. It struck me with great force what an illustration this was of her helplessness, how she had to sit there with tears running down her face. There was nothing she could do about it. She could not even wipe them away.'

54

# NATIONAL LIFE

Elizabeth was fortunate that she was taken to the National Hospital for Nervous Diseases not only because new respiratory equipment was being developed there but because of the eccentric nature of the place, or rather the eccentric natures of some of the people who worked there. The hospital, which is famous throughout the world for its neurological research, treatment of nervous system disorders and brain surgery, had an odd beginning.

In Victorian times the house which stood on the site was owned by two spinster sisters. One day they were looking out of their window into Queen Square when they saw a man fall down outside their door in the throes of an epileptic fit. They sent their servants to carry the sufferer inside and when he had recovered they questioned him about his disease and its treatment. He replied that there was no treatment and no hospital in London catered for epileptics. His words had a profound effect on the Christian-hearted ladies and before long they turned their home into the first hospital to deal with such cases, much to the indignation of the neighbours who could see the value of their properties falling as a stream of epileptics — mostly from the lower orders — invaded the sanctity of Queen Square.

The sisters were mindful of the difficulties epileptics had in obtaining and holding employment, and when they bequeathed their home to a hospital trust one of the conditions was that whenever possible the ward maids should be recruited from epileptics. When Elizabeth was in the hospital a score of these girls worked there and the following conversation was not unusual:

'Has anybody seen Jessie?'

'She's having a fit, Sister.'

'I do hope she put the tea tray down first.'

The Matron, Miss Margery Ling, is the idol of these girls, indeed their veneration is probably similar to that felt by the troops in the Crimea for Florence Nightingale. It is Matron who generates the curious spirit of warmth and humour which pervades the National, though this does not mean she is easy-going in essential management of the hospital. If anything is not up to the strict standard required for an internationally revered medical establishment, her wrath can be Olympian. The remarkable thing about her is her ablity to find time to spend with patients as though each was the only one she has to care for, and when she continues on her round there lingers behind a comforting aura of calm.

'Patients before starch' could be her motto. When I was an orderly in the National I experienced a typical example of this. In a private room on a ward there was a charming elderly patient dying of cancer. He had a country estate and we affectionately nicknamed him 'the last of the squires' as he seemed to possess all the virtues of an old-world gentleman — humour, courage and courtesy to the most menial. In his cupboard he kept a stock of champagne and, though he was forbidden to take it himself, he invited members of the staff in for a drink when they were going off duty, smiling like a gracious host when they raised their glasses in his direction.

As I got to know him he said the one regret he had was that he would not be seeing his old retriever Glory before the end came.

'Not that old Glory will be long behind me,' he said. 'Had him since he was tiny pup, one of the best pals I ever had.'

It seemed that something should be done about this, and plans were laid. The next Sunday afternoon I went down to Queen Square where a pre-war Rolls Royce was parked. The elderly chauffeur gave me the lead of an equally elderly and obese dog, and I took Glory up to the ward in the service lift. Luckily no one was about as I led him to his master's room and once he had waddled inside I hastily shut the door. The thought of Sister's reaction if she learned that I had smuggled an animal into her ward was something I did not care to dwell on. Thank goodness she had Sunday afternoon off.

Glory immediately went to the bed and looked up at his master's face with adoring eyes while his tongue licked the emaciated hand which hung down over the counterpane.

The delight the two had in their clandestine meeting made me pray to whatever gods there are that the after life is not just the prerogative of the human species, that on some Elysian Field Glory and his master would once again range over the flower-starred grass.

With these thoughts I left them to take round afternoon tea to the rest of the patients. Half an hour later I returned to escort the dog back to the car for his return journey to Herefordshire. The corridor was clear and everything was going well when Glory evinced a desire to cock his leg against the spotless wall.

'Hold on, boy,' I hissed desperately, tugging at his lead. And at that moment my blood ran chill as round the corner of the corridor appeared two surgeons with white coats flying in the wake of Matron. The sight of Glory trying to balance on three legs froze them to a halt but Matron bustled on towards us.

'Mr Alexander, I think that doggie would be happier outside,' she said brightly, leading the two doctors out of sight before they could regain their speech.

I dragged Glory to the lift and he was back on his way in the Rolls within a minute and then I waited for the message for me to report to Matron's office. But the summons never came — she understood.

A piece of hospital folklore about Matron concerns her habit of taking walking patients, or epileptic ward maids, for a spin in her veteran Rolls Royce tourer. Apparently she was driving a party of these maids round Eros in Piccadilly Circus when the motor failed, which was the signal for the girls to throw fits. The picture of Miss Ling coping with a broken-down car full of convulsed passengers in the midst of London traffic is a picture dear to her staff.

Elizabeth soon found she had a firm friend in Matron who did everything she could think of to combat the black depression which would sometimes overtake the girl in the lung. When she found her with unwipable tears on her cheeks she would reach for a bottle of sherry in Elizabeth's locker.

'Have a little of Matron's medicine, dear,' she would say, pouring some into a special spouted cup. 'It'll do you good.'

Sometimes she would stage a one-woman singing performance for Elizabeth, accompanying the words with comical gestures. *There Was An Old Woman* and *Count Your Blessings* were her star numbers. She also tried — alas unsuccessfully — to fix the wing mirror of a car on Elizabeth's windowsill so that she could watch a pair of blue tits which came for crumbs there.

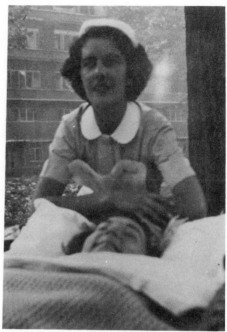

*Nurse Jenny Poynting — now Mrs Ripley — the night special who Matron 'forgot to take off'*

One day when Elizabeth was suffering from the kidney stone Matron appeared with a large bouquet of blue and pink sweet-peas. They were from the Duke of Kent who was in another ward under observation following a car crash and who had been told about the paralysed dancer. Elizabeth was too ill to say thank you, but Matron reported to His Highness that the patient had been delighted with them. Another kindness was when Matron saw a friendship develop between Elizabeth and Nurse Jenny Poynting who was the 'night special'. Because of this closeness between patient and nurse, Miss Ling 'forgot' to take her off night duty for twelve months.

In talking to the author while this book was being written Miss Ling said how, out of the thousands of patients who had passed through her care in the last twenty-five years, Elizabeth stood out.

'She only survived because she had the discipline of the artist,' she said. 'She has that "extra sensitivity" which is one of the things which sustains people through their blackest hours. With her artistic abilities she had a lot to give, and over the years she certainly has given a lot.'

\* \* \*

The other great National character Elizabeth remembers with affection and gratitude was one of the hospital almoners Sheridan Russell. Everything about him was unusual, his background, his approach to his work (he was the first male almoner), and his quirky sense of humour. Above all Elizabeth felt a rapport with him because he was a fellow artist — Sheridan Russell was, and still is, a brilliant 'cellist.

As a boy he wanted to become a professional musician, but·his father told him that it would be better to become a first-rate farmer than a second-rate 'cellist.

'When I proved to him I was a third-rate farmer I returned to being a second-rate 'cellist,' he says. 'I also became secretary of an organisation for the protection of animals in Italy, and I travelled about that country introducing humane slaughter methods in abattoirs. During the first part of the Second World War I was cryptoanalyst at a hush-hush establishment in Bletchley. Then because of my experience of the country, I became a British Liason Officer with the partisans in Italy for two-and-a-half years.

'When the war ended I wanted to do something interesting, something which involved people, so I took a course for almoners, which up until then had been restricted to women, and I started at the National. I remember the pay was shocking. I was earning £100 a year less than a

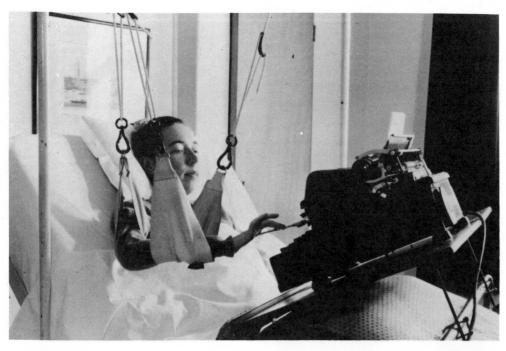

*Learning to type*

clerk until the hospital secretary put me down on the books as one, but I found it fascinating work.

'Looking back on all the people I dealt with I remember Elizabeth as a unique case because she has such guts, she's a fighter and she *minds* terribly... she's been deeply hurt and unhappy but she has something which most people haven't got whether ill or not.

'Quite frankly, I wanted her to die when she was so ill. I hoped she would and I remember when she was having a very bad time and her doctor worked round the clock on her for two or three days. I said to him, "I know you've worked very hard but..." And he replied, "That isn't for me to decide, is it?"'

'Poor child, I thought, what life is there for her? But I was wrong because there has been a life for her, she made her own life. So often since then I have wished I could have introduced Elizabeth to other severely disabled patients to show them the possibility of making a life for themselves, though of course people have guts or they haven't — you can't teach guts, can you?'

Sheridan had various ways of helping Elizabeth but basically he wanted her to feel that he really cared about her situation, and to make her laugh.

'I hated the thought of telling her I was going on holiday,' he recalls. 'I though it might depress her to say I was going to Venice when she was locked in the lung. So I used to write to her saying how ghastly it all was — how the food was terrible and the streets were absolutely flooded...'

Elizabeth remembers Sheridan for the unexpected things he did. One lunch time he walked into her room and gave her an hour-long recital of Bach on his 'cello, ending the performance by presenting her with a bouquet. And it was Sheridan who introduced her to the idea of using an electric typewriter. Such machines were expensive and not so common as they are today but somehow he talked the Westminster Bank into lending Elizabeth one.

At this time she was able to spend short periods out of the lung, breathing independently with her neck muscles. This gave her physiotherapist a chance to try and develop movement in other parts of her body, but the only tiny response was in her right arm. A sling was suspended over Elizabeth's bed and with her arm supported in this way she was able to move it slightly to and fro. It was this movement which gave Sheridan the idea of the typewriter, which in turn gave Elizabeth an incentive because until then there seemed little purpose in merely swinging her arm.

A stick was attached to her hand and the sling was adjusted so that it would be possible to press the keys with it. The learning process was extremely slow, the biggest obstacle being that Elizabeth found it difficult to concentrate on two things at once — hitting the correct letter *and* breathing. In fact it took years before she could perform both functions simultaneously.

Sheridan encouraged her by sending zany letters, often in scroll form so that they could be unfolded before her eyes while she lay in the lung, to which he expected typed replies. These often began with such greetings as 'DEAD MTRUSSEL.'

'While I was on the rocking bed he wrote me a most extraordinary letter,' Elizabeth recalls. 'It was in the form of an S-shaped scroll so that as I rocked I was supposed to be able to read it. He is delightfully dotty and a beautiful 'cellist though he was never too proud to help produce the music for the hospital pantomime. With people like him and Matron to support me I did not realise the uniqueness of the hospital until I left it. There was always a very relaxed, peaceful atmosphere about the place with its gentle routine. During the early weeks of crisis my only visitors were my parents and my sister Janet who was still a patient there, but all the staff went out of their way to make me feel as at home as possible.'

* * *

When Elizabeth was admitted to the National Hospital news of her illness stunned the ballet world, that a dancer should be completely paralysed from the neck down seemed so horrible and unjust. Flowers arrived every day and once visiting was permitted Elizabeth was never allowed to feel she had been forgotten by her friends and well-wishers. Many of her old dancing colleagues came to see her but they were mostly men — the girls could not trust themselves to keep their composure at the sight of her in the sinister-looking tank.

Of the tokens of love and encouragement which arrived at that time two in particular remain in her memory — a posy of flowers from the children she taught and a bridal bouquet from Dame Margot Fonteyn. She was getting married the next day and two of the boys from the ballet company came round from Covent Garden with a beautiful arrangement of flowers which had been given to her for her wedding.

Another thoughtful gesture was made by Dr Hierons who looked after Elizabeth when she was first admitted. One evening he brought his wife to Elizabeth's room. Both were in evening dress and he explained, as he placed his buttonhole in a little vase for her, 'We came because you

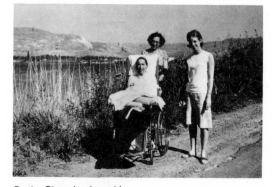

*By the River Jordan with Janet Harvey and Sheila Forster*

59

must be so tired of seeing people in uniform.'

Several hospital padres visited Elizabeth and she found the most helpful were those who never mentioned religion unless they brought Holy Communion.

'The ones I liked best were those I could have a jolly good laugh with because humour is a very important factor when you are ill,' she says. 'I don't really like people praying over me — I find it embarrassing. There was one chaplain who invariably put his foot in it as far as I was concerned. Whenever he said goodbye he would add some tactless remark like "May you soon be dancing round the Maypole again." It was hardly the thing to encourage someone who was permanently paralysed. I was still acutely sensitive and little things like this would upset me for hours.

On the question of religion Elizabeth is reserved. To her it seems to be a very private matter, but she does say that she is religious.

'I think unconsciously it has helped to sustain me,' she says today. 'I believe that deep down it is one of the reasons I am not bitter. I think God is infinitely compassionate and when I look at my life I can see that nothing that has happened to me has been wasted. I'm incredibly fortunate — in spite of all that's wrong with me — because I'm surrounded by friends who are only too anxious to help and a family that stood by me and backed me, and in my position I probably see the best side of most people. I have discovered gifts which I didn't know existed, and I don't even know if they were there before my illness, but I'm sure if I hadn't become paralysed I would never have used them. I am sometimes asked how I reconcile my position — lying here immobilized — with an all-embracing God. My answer is that I think there is a purpose behind it, but if it is only to teach me patience it is quite a hard way of going about it!'

Elizabeth admits that the greatest disappointment due to her paralysis was that it made marriage and children out of the question, and she feels it was fortunate that she was not engaged when she was stricken with polio.

\* \* \*

In her small room Elizabeth felt remote from the outside world. All she could see of it was the square of her window reflected in the angled mirror above her head and when she occasionally glimpsed the white habits of the nuns from the nearby Italian Hospital it somehow emphasised her isolation. Then one pleasant Sunday morning, when Queen Square was full of the Sabbath stillness which is such a curious and delightful aspect of the city, it was decided she should have her first outing since she had been hospitalized.

She was lifted from the lung on to an operating theatre trolley and under the care of a doctor, a physiotherapist and two nurses she was taken down in the lift and wheeled into the outside air. There is always a magic moment when one leaves a hospital after a long time; the air is sweeter than usual, the green of the trees and the blue of the sky is more vivid and there is an awareness of detail — the eye of a sparrow or the pattern of foliage which one never noticed before. Lying on the trolley Elizabeth gazed up at the walls of the hospital and it seemed that at every window there were hands waving to her. Her temporary release meant a great deal to a lot of people.

After that people who arrived early in Queen Square frequently saw Elizabeth being wheeled round it for her 'constitutional.' Once, when she saw an onlooker staring at her charge, a nurse explained, 'She's just recovering from the birth of still-born twins!' Often Jenny Poynting, after finishing her twelve-hour night shift, would have breakfast and then return to take her friend out. A hideous Victorian wicker spinal carriage with a 'revolting' black hood was found in the cellar of the hospital and this took the place of the theatre trolley. One doctor swore it had come back from the Crimea with Florence Nightingale but at least it gave Elizabeth a feeling of freedom after the imprisonment in the iron lung.

And it was in this contraption—which prompted a little girl to say, 'Mummy, look at that lady in her pram!'—that Elizabeth fulfilled her first social engagement since becoming paralysed. Her friends at Coram Fields had not forgotten her, and an invitation had come to the hospital for her to attend the opening of a new band room there by Lady Cynthia Colville. As the time approached Elizabeth became more and more nervous. To be wheeled round Queen Square was one thing, to go to a public function quite another. There are two other hospitals in Queen Square apart from the National and the sight of wheelchairs and patients being assisted on their slow walks by nurses is quite the normal thing there. Thus Elizabeth never felt that she stood out from the rest, but to be the only paralytic among a gathering of healthy people was a different matter. And, while Elizabeth was in Queen Square, there was always the comforting bulk of the National looming above her should anything go wrong.

On the day of the opening she felt her courage wane. At lunchtime she told her doctor that she could not face the ordeal. Jenny Poynting persuaded her to change her mind for, with kindly forethought which so frequently lifts the nursing profession out of the routine of bedpans and dressings, she had arranged for Ken, one of Elizabeth's ex-dancing partners, to come and push the Crimean carriage. As a result of Jenny's arguments—and the sudden and delightful appearance of Ken—Elizabeth agreed to go through with it. There was much laughter and excitement as one of the nurses applied cosmetics to her face for the Great Outing. Then, with a Beaverometer hidden under her feet in case of emergency, Ken began wheeling the carriage in the direction of Coram's Fields. The ancient vehicle seemed to have a wilful mind of its own, perhaps its Victorian canes disapproved of the levity which surrounded it on such an august occasion but it did everything it could to end up in the gutter. Ken made the most of this and by the time the erratic journey was completed Elizabeth could hardly breathe for laughing.

Thanks to the buoyant company of Jenny and Ken she found that her fears had been groundless. Lord Esher greeted her with a bouquet and the dancing pupils clamoured to see her; Press photographers raised their cameras and such was the animation around her that she did not have time to reflect that the last time this had happened she had been on the stage...

The combination of excitement and shallow breathing caused Elizabeth to become flushed, and this worried a fellow guest.

'Don't worry, I have a breathing machine under my feet,' Elizabeth reassured her.

'Oh!' exclaimed the lady. 'I didn't know they could breathe you that way nowadays.

In trying to keep a straight face Elizabeth really did become breathless, but when she was lifted back into the iron lung after the reception she had a great sense of elation. A Russian proverb says that a journey of a thousand miles begins with a single step, and Elizabeth knew she had taken that step.

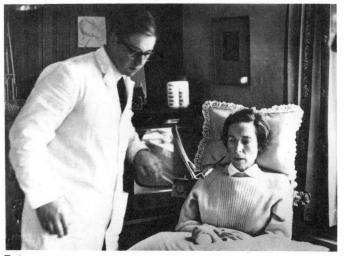

*Trying out environmental
control under
Roger Jefcoate's guidance*

# IN LIMBO

It was a sad day—and the first of many to follow. After two-and-a-quarter years Elizabeth was to leave the National. She had reached the point where nothing more could be done for her, and such is the highly specialized work of the establishment that once the curing period is over patients must make way for others who not only come from all parts of the British Isles but from the world over. No other hospital would accept Elizabeth until she could be independent of a breathing machine for three to four hours at a time. Now that goal had been reached and she was to be transferred to the Royal National Orthopaedic Hospital at Stanmore.

'You must think of the National as your second home,' Matron told her on the morning of her departure. 'You will always be welcome to come back if the necessity should arise.'

When the ambulance pulled up outside the main entrance a large crowd of staff and patients was there to give Elizabeth a noisy and affectionate farewell, and she found that Sheridan Russell had organised a red carpet for her to be wheeled over. This was not just a parting gesture to a popular patient—it was because she had come to mean more to the staff than she herself realised, from Matron and the consultants down to the maids who would proudly tell new patients about 'Miss Iggins who had been a belly dancer.' They had seen her brought in under the shadow of death, they had seen her cyanosed and they had followed her progress literally breath by breath as she fought to become independent of life support equipment. When she succeeded in typing a few lines word went round the wards; when she was suffering from one of he black depressions it would be reported in the staff dining room, 'Elizabeth is having a bad day today.'

Interest in the progress of a patient is the fascination of nursing, and few lay people realise what it means to hospital staff to see a patient they have nursed back to health walk out to resume his or her place in the outside world. It is one up against the common enemy—it is the justification for the long hours of swotting, the aching feet and the jobs which would make other workers scream for 'dirty money', 'danger money', 'unsociable hours money' and bonuses for responsibility. Compared with shorthand typists and secretaries, nurses are financially second-class citizens, but at least they do have their moments of job satisfaction.

There was less of this satisfaction at the National because of the specialist nature of its work. Usually patients arrive there from general hospitals for advanced treatment—operations for brain tumours, for example—and, when this is completed, are returned for general nursing. But with a patient like Elizabeth the staff had time to get involved. She was so long at the National that she had become an institution; nurses taking the special neurological course at Queen Square found her there when they arrived and she was still there when they left. Thus, on the day of departure, many staff members felt that things would never be quite the same with Elizabeth gone. Such was the size and ardour of the send-off as Elizabeth was lifted into the ambulance that a distracted motorist drove straight into one of its doors. When a new vehicle had been procured Elizabeth was driven away in company with a doctor and her good friend Nurse Ilona Skobisova who had originally come from Prague. A riot of thoughts raced through her mind. Her only experience of hospitals had been the National, apart from those Christmas visits to Great Ormond Street which she had dreaded so much. And although she herself was now disabled, she still had that childhood aversion to illness and deformity—and the thought of hospitals.

At Queen Square she had been accustomed to a room of her own where she could have the solace of music whenever she felt like it, where Matron permitted visitors at any hour and where nurses and orderlies came to chat in their free moments. The thought of being in a general ward filled her with misgiving. No matter how ill she had felt in the past she had been able to retain her individuality but from now on she would be one of a score of patients. The days when the matron would cheer her up with an extempore song-and-dance were over.

Her feeling about the National was later summed up when it was suggested she should undertake a pilgrimage to Lourdes.

'Why should I?' she replied. 'My miracle has already happened—I'm alive. I believe that if I had not been taken to the National I would have died. I went there by chance—or was it? That hospital and its staff were my miracle!'

\* \* \*

In that darkening February day the Stanmore hospital looked particularly bleak as the ambulance passed through its iron gates and parked outside the Administration Block. There was a long wait, then it was off again down a concrete track between rows of old army huts which were used as wards. Later Ilona told her friends at the National, 'Poor Elizabeth, she will not be happy in those cowsheds.'

The vehicle halted at Hut 8. There was another wait while a trolley was brought and then Elizabeth was wheeled into what—after her small room—seemed an enormous ward with twenty beds lining its walls.

The iron lung she would use was just inside the door, and she realised with a pang of fear that the orthopaedic staff then on duty had no experience of breathing machines. Ilona had to settle her inside the tank and, with the doctor's help, set the controls before saying goodbye. When they left Elizabeth had never before suffered such loneliness.

Looking back on this traumatic experience much later on she wrote: 'Having been "specialled" until now, I was missing the seclusion of my room at the National. I would have to get used to it, however, as life was now going to be very different. Looking back, I realise that this toughening-up process was vital to my rehabilitation, but at the time it seemed cruel and I admit I was sorry for myself. There were far fewer nurses in attendance and I became very aware of my helplessness and complete dependence on other people.'

After the peace of her own room Elizabeth found the public ward so noisy she could not think properly, only reflect unhappily on how completely her life had altered. What a relief she felt when it came time for lights out and she could briefly escape into the privacy of darkness!

Next morning she discovered that her routine began at a quarter past five when she was given a tepid wash and had her pressure areas rubbed with surgical spirit to prevent bedsores, always a threat to those immobilised in bed. When this was completed the ward was roused and Elizabeth had to lie for a couple of hours gazing into space until a nurse came and fed her breakfast. Morning and afternoon she was wheeled by a porter to the Treatment Block for physiotherapy. At three-thirty she learned to her dismay that her teeth were given their final brush for the day.

On the more positive side Elizabeth found that her fellow patients were kind and sympathetic, and those who could walk would give her drinks when required or turn the leaf of her book. Reading in the iron lung was a frustrating business as the open book was laid on a piece of perspex above her face and she had to rely on the availability and goodwill of others when she came to the end of a page.

'The Stanmore physiotherapists were most understanding about my problems and depressions,' she wrote, 'but it took many years to fully accept the fact that I had been irrevocably immobilised. The odds seemed too great. I had black days when I despaired of ever doing anything with my life. On these days I remained in the ward, unable to face the ever cheerful physios and the jolly atmosphere that always prevailed in their department. I longed for solitude. I did not want sympathy, I just wanted to be left alone.'

* * *

No matter how depressing things were for Elizabeth there were odd moments of humour. Her favourite hospital anecdote concerns the night she was dressed in a shroud.

'My nightie had accidentally been sent off to the laundry and the only alternative they had to offer was an uncomfortable much laundered wincyette thing, which the nurses knew would irritate my skin,' she relates. 'The softest thing they had on the ward was a shroud, made of paper. They are really not too bad to look at and I had just been put into one when the Ward Sister came in to say Goodnight. She looked at me rather oddly as I sat in my chair. I was afraid that the nurse who had dressed me would get into trouble, so I said brightly, "It isn't a very good fit, is it, Sister?"

'She looked again and, realising what was going on, started to laugh. She laughed so much she had to leave the room.

'In the middle of the night I woke up — sweat absolutely pouring off me. I rang my bell and said to the nurse, "I'm dreadfully hot, do you think it's the shroud I'm wearing?" She was Irish and terribly superstitious and in an outraged voice she cried, "You're what? I'd never have put you in one of those." I said, "Do you think you could get someone to help you open the lung and take the thing off me?" She called another nurse and they tore great chunks out of it, hoping this would do the trick. When they had finished their work of destruction, they clamped me in again. The assistant nurse said with complete seriousness, "Funny! Nobody has ever complained before."'

Twice weekly Elizabeth had an occupational therapy session in which the therapist tried to get her to stencil tiles. Her arm was suspended in a sling, as it was for typing, and a paint brush was fastened to her fingers. It

was guided in the direction of a paint pot; then, when the brush was full, she swung her arm and tried to splosh colour on the tile. Usually the paint went everywhere but on it.

When several tiles had been stencilled in this hit-or-miss manner they were taken away to be fired and the following week she saw the results. Those around her praised them and said how artistic she was — lies which were told out of kindness to encourage her. The fact was that the results were horrible and Elizabeth knew it. Apart from everything else, the colours changed in the firing and now looked utterly drab. Even today Elizabeth gives a mental shudder when she remembers those tiles; then she felt she no more had an artistic future than she did as the little girl who was permitted to do sewing instead of artwork.

* * *

When Elizabeth was admitted to Stanmore it was known definitely that she could expect no further improvement, that she would remain paralysed for the rest of her life. The object of her stay at the orthopaedic hospital was for her to be physically strengthened as much as possible. Until then she had been motivated by the thought of improving her bodily condition by weaning herself from the Beaverometer and trying to increase the daily score of breaths taken independently of mechanical help. But now — what? At this point she knew that she could never progress, that dancing and teaching were dead to her, and that always she would be dependent on others.

Seeing the effect of long-term hospitalization on many patients, Elizabeth had a dread of becoming like them — a dread of seeing the walls of the ward as the horizons of the world, of giving up one's mind to the endless telly-watching and of becoming a 'perfect patient' from a hospital's view point. Such a person is one who makes no fuss nor demands out-of-the-ordinary favours, and who above all has an attitude of almost simple-minded acceptance. When one considers the problems which beset modern hospitals, coupled with the traditional view that efficiency is in direct ratio to uniformity, it is easy to understand why the conforming patient is so welcome in many establishments, and conversely why the 'outsider' is always suspect.

That Elizabeth was not regarded as a perfect patient was later demonstrated when a journalist 'writing her up' was allowed to see a hospital report on her. He told Elizabeth that it was highly critical of her because she 'regretted the past'. It seems incredible that someone who had been a successful dancer before becoming permanently incapacitated should be expected not to regret the past!

'The patient satisfied with a cabbage-like existence is usually far more popular than one with ambition and drive,' says Elizabeth. 'So often those in charge do not understand what lies behind this fighting spirit. To them we appear difficult, demanding and an incredible nuisance. This battle against conflicting forces can easily wear you down, and it takes a ruthless determination to reach the goal you have set yourself.'

To get out of hospital, to avoid institutionalization, now became her main aim in life. At the time the possibility of success seemed remote to say the least; it was like a prisoner on Devil's Island dreaming about swimming across the shark-infested sea to freedom. But from now on this book changes from a hospital story to one of escape.

* * *

Thanks to the cuirass-type respirator it became possible for Elizabeth to leave Stanmore for a weekend with her elder sister. As Janet was an ex-nursing sister and her husband David a G.P., the medical authorities must have felt reassured that their patient would be in competent hands.

Elizabeth became so excited at the prospect of a brief respite from ward life that her temperature began to climb on the Friday morning while waiting for the ambulance, but her doctors turned a blind eye to this and soon she was on her way to Hertfordshire.

Despite attending to their three young children, Janet and David were able to look after her perfectly. She had been given a bed in the downstairs living-room and a bell was rigged up which would sound an alarm in case of a problem with her respirator. It was over two-and-a-half years since she had been in a house, had been with people in ordinary clothes rather than medical uniforms, and had enjoyed everyday domestic things which were not governed by necessary routine. The happy hours fled and suddenly it was Sunday evening when she had to return to Stanmore. But she did have the consolation of knowing that this weekend visit, and the others which would follow it, were rehearsals for when she hoped to be able to live with her mother and father — a prospect which held the promise of escape from institutional life.

In the autumn of 1955 an ambulance carried her out of the gates of Stanmore Hospital and bore her south to the Old School House at Mongeham in Kent. Here the dining-room was converted for her use, a district nurse called every morning and a physiotherapist twice a week*.

For Elizabeth it was sheer delight to be reunited with her parents who had given her such loving support since the onset of polio. She found only one jarring note and this was her mother's attitude to her condition, and it demonstrates how the effect of illness is not confined to the patient. Her mother could not reconcile herself to the fact that there would be no further improvement for her daughter.

'My mother would not accept that I had got everything back I was likely to get. She insisted that I was going to make a complete recovery, no matter how many times I told her it was not going to happen. Alison* just would not believe it.'

"My mother would not accept that I had got everything back I was likely to get back,' says Elizabeth. 'She would tell everybody that I was going to make a recovery. No matter how many times I said, "Mummy, it's not going to happen," she would not believe it.'

That winter was a severe one. Elizabeth lived in fear of storms bringing down electric cables and discontinuing the power for her respirator pump. This happened on several occasions and her parents had to get her out of the lung immediately no matter what time of day or night. On windy evenings their anxiety prevented them from getting rest and sadly Elizabeth realised that having her in their home was too much for them. Both were now elderly and as she was in her respirator for nineteen hours a day there was a great deal of nursing for them to do despite the help of the visiting nurse.

So much for her dream of escaping from hospital! After Christmas an ambulance arrived at Mongeham to take her away again, and in the next dozen years she was to be admitted to as many different hospitals and medical hostels.

*Alison stayed at home to help her parents look after Elizabeth for many months.

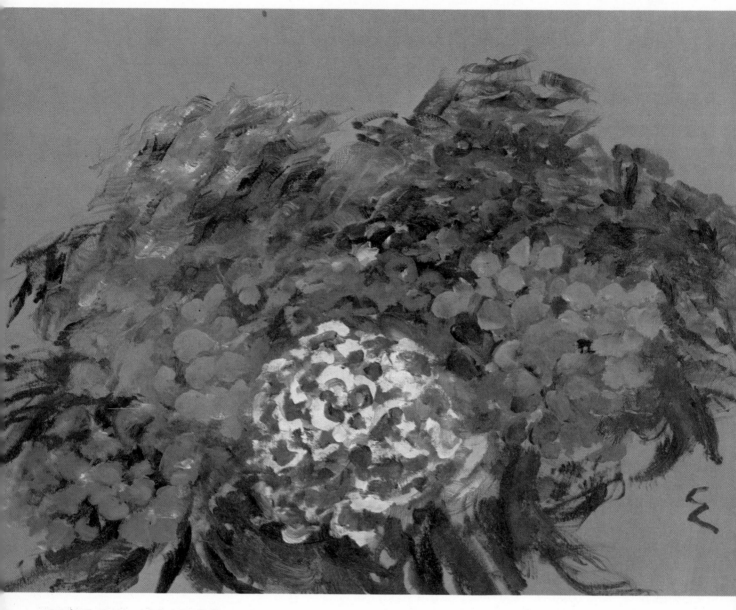

*One of Elizabeth's early flower paintings*

Cunard

# LOW EBB

The National Hospital again.

Matron had kept her word and, when Elizabeth could no longer remain with her parents at Mongeham because of power failures, she invited her back until other arrangements could be made. Although Elizabeth was pleased to be once more among the friends who had looked after her for so long, she was bitterly aware that this return to Queen Square signified the failure of her attempt to live her own life.

To help her to get over this disappointment two lady doctors decided that she should go to the ballet at Covent Garden. The arrangements were made and when the great day arrived those involved were filled with apprehension. Would the memories which the Royal Opera House would revive prove too much for her? The excitement before the curtain went up, the music swelling from the orchestra pit, the ethereal forms floating across the brilliantly-lit world of make-believe... these things had been the very essence of her life but now would they merely underline all that she had lost? Everyone held their breath, including Elizabeth — almost. Her main worry was that she would get so carried away she would forget to breathe.

She spent the day lying quietly in her respirator, gathering her strength for the evening when she would see Margot Fonteyn dance *The Firebird*. Because her wheelchair had to be in place before the audience was admitted to the auditorium, the St John's ambulance whisked her away early. As it pulled up outside the familiar facade a young man stepped forward to welcome her. Arnott was one of her ex-dancing partners and now a member of the Royal Ballet. He seemed so genuinely pleased to see her, chatting continuously as she was carried up the grand staircase to her box, that she did not have time to be engulfed by waves of nostalgia. And during the performance she remembered to use her vital neck muscles despite the beauty of Stravinsky's masterpiece.

When the ambulance returned her to Queen Square the anxious night staff were relieved to see her eyes shining with pure happiness; clearly Elizabeth had forgotten her own predicament in the joy of watching a ballet performance again. The next day a letter came from Dame Margot Fonteyn expressing the hope that she had enjoyed *Firebird*.

It was on this outing that Elizabeth met two of her favourite characters, Sergeant Martin and Mr Posstlethwaite, the top-hatted commissionaires at the Royal Opera House.

'Sergeant Martin — the big one with the bristling moustache — looks as tough as nails but really he's as soft as butter,' says Elizabeth. 'He immediately understood it was my first time there in a wheelchair and that I didn't like being stared at. It's something that can't be helped because you are an oddity, but he did everything he could to put me at ease. "Very cold out there, madam," he said, re-arranging my shawl round my shoulders and standing in such a way that he shielded me from the crowd.

"People can be so thoughtful. When the Moscow Ballet came to London I received a cheque for 1/11½d from the Sadlers Wells Company. The members had had a whip-round to reserve me a box — one cost twenty-five pounds even in those pre-inflation days — for the Russian performance, and the 1/11½d was the amount left over which, they said, was to buy myself a hat!

'I have lost count of the number of times I have been to the theatre since then, but all have been enjoyable. When Sir Frederick Ashton was director of Sadler's Wells he said I could come to any dress rehearsal I liked. What was very sweet was the way some of the boys and girls I used to work with would spot me from the stage and give me a wink over the footlights. Phillip Chatfield and Ronald Hynd, who had trained with me, were amazingly quick at picking me out, and would always manage to give me a special smile. Little things like that meant a great deal.'

'The second time she was taken to the ballet she was visited in her box by Violetta Elvin and David Blair. She had always been an admirer of Violetta and the style of dancing she introduced to London when her author husband Harold brought her from Moscow, and she was delighted when the ballerina presented her with one of her autographed ballet shoes. That night the nurses hung it above Elizabeth's bed in the Hendon Isolation Hospital where she was staying at the time.

'Humph!' exclaimed the Medical Superintendent when he saw it. 'She might have given you a new one while she was at it!'

\* \* \*

Elizabeth could not remain for long at the National, and soon she began a seemingly-endless period of being transferred to establishment after establishment. Her problem was that she did not fit into any convenient category.

Looking back to that time, she has written, 'I was shunted from hospital to hospital, on to the family, then back again into hospital. I suffered an overwhelming sense of uselessness and must have been a very difficult person. Kind friends tried to invent gadgets to make me more independent, but I had so little movement that these usually ended up by being tremendously elaborate pieces of equipment which the staff had no time to fix. These lay idle, cluttering up the ward, and I was a most unpopular patient as a result.'

Certainly in a few instances — a very few when one considers the hundreds of people who have been involved in Elizabeth's welfare — she found herself at odds with some individual member of the nursing staff. The worst case — and one that those who know Elizabeth

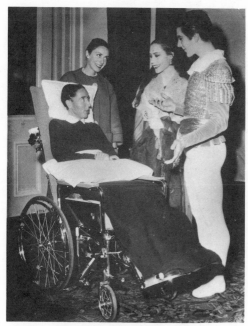

*In the crush bar with Annette Page,*
*Svetlana Beriosova and Donald MacCleary*

*Karen Perry rehearsing for Elizabeth*

believe left its mark on her — concerned a sister who took an intense dislike to her when she was brought under her care. One of the reasons may have been that the sister had a morbid fear of poliomyelitis though, of course, there was no question of Elizabeth being infectious.

To begin with Elizabeth was placed at the far end of the ward although respiratory polio patients are supposed to be close to the door for safety reasons. The fact that the nurses were forbidden to talk to her was just one of the irritations she had to suffer — and to a paralysed person such irritations are hardly minor.

'Feed her and don't speak to her,' was Sister's edict.

'She used to leave me lying on my tummy until my face was puce from breathlessness,' Elizabeth recalls. 'It is then when you realise your total dependence upon people. As far as I knew I had never done anything to this sister but she was cruel in every possible way. Staff Nurse became so worried about her behaviour towards me that she would say to the nurses, "Hurry up and look after Elizabeth while I keep Sister talking in the office." In the end everything became so unendurable that I asked to be removed from the ward, or if that was not possible, from the hospital. It seems that when I left Sister transferred her malice to a Hungarian lady whose bed had been opposite mine. The poor thing had a nervous breakdown within three months.'

There is a belief that suffering does — or should — make people patient or even saintly. Therefore Elizabeth is sometimes regarded as though she has an invisible halo, but she would agree that suffering in itself has no virtue — it is one's reaction to it which counts. The fact is that patients are still people, their illness may add to their difficulties, may embitter them or give them a better insight into life, but it does not automatically ennoble them.

One of the wisest things said to Elizabeth by her father was, 'Never forget you are exactly the same as everyone else, except for the fact you cannot move.' On the face of it an obvious remark and yet it is a truth which is often difficult for both patients and nursing staff to remember. There is something about hospitals which begins to alter the perspective of their inmates from the moment they are admitted. This is not a criticism of hospitals or their dedicated nursing personnel; it is a process which happens when people are immobilised and concentration on their physical state leaves their mental side without stimulation. The result can be that the evening menu, or the debate over which television channel to watch, assumes an importance which would be laughable in normal circumstances. Another aspect of this is the compulsion to be bright about everything no matter what the circumstances.

How many really poorly patients respond to the routine greeting of 'How are we this morning?' with 'Fine, Sister, fine!' There is a conviction that to admit just how miserable one is would be a breach of good manners.

What the author of this book admires about Elizabeth above all else is the way she has fought to retain her personality. It is something which at times makes her appear difficult, especially to those who have known her for only a short period.

This question of being difficult worries her. She says that she probably is, but feels she is sometimes misjudged because of the nature of her disability. For example, after a day of breathing with her neck muscles she is low on oxygen, and so she cuts down on the number of words she uses which makes her sound curt, especially to anyone who expects her to be effusive. On occasions she may seem impatient when someone is performing a task for her. This is because one of the effects of her body becoming immobilised is that her brain has quickened. It is as though she is on a different time scale to the rest of us, and often the actions of

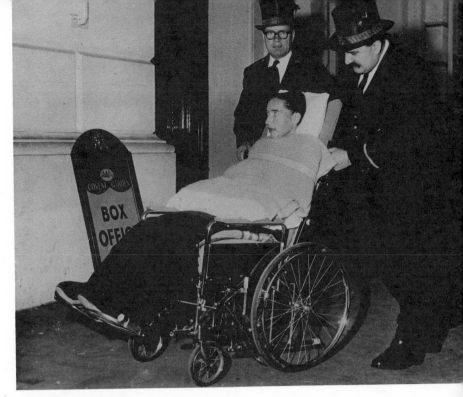

*Entering Covent Garden with Sergeant Martin and Mr Postlethwaite in 1961*

the able-bodied about her appear almost to be in slow motion.

And then, as everyone who knows her agrees, Elizabeth is a perfectionist. As a dancer she never spared herself to achieve some movement; today she is her own severest critic as far as her work is concerned. Thus if she expects meticulousness from herself it follows that she expects it from others.

The view of the author, who once nursed Elizabeth, is that she is not a difficult person — would nurses who looked after her twenty-five years ago still make the journey to Chelmsford to visit her if she was? — rather, she is an impatient one. She feels that so much time is taken up with the chores of disability that every minute of her free time is precious.

\* \* \*

In 1957 Elizabeth arrived at the British Polio Fellowship Hostel. It was yet another situation in which she would have to get to know a completely new set of people and adapt to unaccustomed routines. At this point psychologically she was at one of the lowest ebbs she was ever to reach as a quadraplegic. There was nothing she could do now to improve herself physically and her wish for a more independent life seemed to have been replaced by the prospect of successive institutions. Looking back on that negative period, she comments, 'I was desperately depressed at this time because everything seemed so pointless. I suppose I was suffering from self-pity but there was no end in sight, nothing to strive for.'

At the hostel Elizabeth's mood of dejection was not helped by the fact that during the afternoons there were no staff members on duty which meant she could only spend her time gazing at the ceiling. Once again she was acutely aware of her dependence on others, even for such small things as the turning of the page of her book. Two paralysed fellow residents overcame the problem by mouth sticks. Until then she had rejected any suggestion of using an implement held in her mouth because she feared it would interfere with her breathing — and make her appear ridiculous! Now out of desperation she tried a reading stick. It was difficult to manage but the need was great and she persevered until, to her surprise, she found that she could still breathe with it clamped between her teeth.

*Elizabeth's painting of her "The Gloria" liturgical ballet*

Different sticks were tried until she found one which suited her, a very light rod with a rubber thimble at one end. After a lot of practice she was able to read a book without looking for help every few minutes. To Elizabeth it was an achievement of the greatest importance *as it was the first time in over four years that she could do anything for herself.* Only the pages of glossy magazines remained—and still do—unturnable.

To Elizabeth the value of the achievement was that from then on those long periods of doing nothing were over, but as things were to turn out the real victory was in utilising the part of her body over which she still had control.

The residents of the hostel were fortunate in having the support of an association of voluntary 'Friends' who did everything they could to make life interesting for them. A couple of afternoons a week ladies from the association came to spend time with the patients, and one named Rosie showed Elizabeth an oil painting set which had been donated.

'Why don't you try painting?' she asked. 'I'm sure you could hold a brush in your mouth now that you've got used to the reading stick.'

Elizabeth looked over to where two paralysed patients were engrossed in their artwork—Vicky, who had the use of her hands, was completing a still life and John, a brush held in his teeth, was engrossed in a seascape. Memories returned of the hideous tiles she had tried to paint with her swinging hand at Stanmore and of her childhood aversion to drawing but Rosie seemed so anxious for her to try.

'I'll have a go,' she said doubtfully. Immediately Rosie placed a table in front of her and set up a reading stand against a wobbly pile of books. A canvas board was put into position and she looked at Elizabeth expectantly.

'There! What are you going to paint?'

Elizabeth gazed at the blank board but its pristine whiteness gave no inspiration. There must be something she could paint; John seemed to be getting a lot of satisfaction out of his rolling waves.

'Um—I'll try a landscape.'

'Splendid,' enthused Rosie. 'We'll start with the sky.' She squeezed worms of blue and white paint on to the palette and began mixing them with oil and turpentine.

'Now, we want a touch of red.'

Red? For the sky? thought Elizabeth. She's crazy!

But Rosie added a spot of alizarin to the mixture and suddenly there was a sky colour. It made Elizabeth realise that she knew absolutely nothing about painting. Meanwhile her mentor filled a brush with paint and placed the other end between her teeth. The brush waved wildly not being able to reach the canvas.

'Soon fix that,' declared Rosie and she pushed the pile of books within range. For a moment they tottered and then cascaded to the floor while paint splattered in all directions.

The effort had taken so much out of Elizabeth that she had to give up, but after a cup of tea and half-an-hour's rest she was game to try again. Brush in mouth, she regarded the mocking square of canvas.

'I'll show you!' she told it mentally and, chewing viciously at the wood, dabbled blue on to it. Slowly the paint began to hide that annoying whiteness—until she bit right through the handle. With the shortened brush she had to get close to the 'painting', for her eyes crossed and she became flushed with exertion. When the board was moved back for her inspection she saw that her sky looked ghastly—'like the work of an artistic chimpanzee,' she said later. But—despite the exertion and the mess—it had been fun. She would try again.

An odour of turps soon began to cling to Elizabeth. Her helpers were frequently decorated with multicoloured paint spots (the result of the brush jerking out of control), while she got more colour on herself than on the canvas.

Weeks went by. Then one afternoon she found herself gazing at her first complete picture which she entitled *Three tomatoes on a Wedgwood blue plate.*

'This was painted entirely from imagination and must have started off accidentally,' Elizabeth wrote later. 'My helper at this time was Kit. She mixed the colours, and I expect made a nice tomato red one day. That triggered off the whole thing. The Wedgwood blue plate was my idea and I remember getting very excited as she gradually got the exact colour I had in mind. I had no idea then how to obtain different colours, and it was wonderful for me to find someone who could interpret my ideas so exactly. It was a unique partnership at a very opportune moment, as our artistic feeling and taste seemed to merge.'

Some weeks after the completion of the picture the warden said to Elizabeth, 'We've arranged for you to go to a private nursing home.' She was stunned by this bald announcement which apparently resulted from staff shortage and the inability of the hostel to keep residents who could not look after themselves.

'But—what will that cost?' she asked.

'Twenty-eight pounds a week.'

'I'm sorry, I can't afford it. Please telephone my father and explain the situation.

'There's no alternative.'

'Then please telephone Miss Ling at the National.'

So once again her possessions and life support apparatus were packed, an ambulance arrived and she was on her way to the security of Queen Square. Here the occupational therapist Dorothy Cockayne decided to do everything she could to foster her new found interest. Elizabeth has described Dorothy as 'an aesthetic, delicate-looking person who has suffered severe illnesses, including a long period of blindness.' Having known what it was like to be dependent on other people, Dorothy had deep understanding of Elizabeth's problems.

The first thing was to design an easel which would fit on the arms of her wheelchair. Mounted in front of it were four pots containing white, blue, red and yellow paint, all of which had a tendency to turn to a uniform mud hue because Elizabeth had no means of cleaning her brushes. But what fun she had. At last she was doing something creative even though the results fell ludicrously short of her critical goal.

Again Elizabeth had to move, the National being unable to keep her. For three weeks she stayed in a Cheshire Home where, without her gentle tutor, she struggled to paint on her own, mainly little pictures of fish swimming amongst reeds. Then one day in February, 1958, she was taken to the National Hospital Convalescent Home in Finchley. Here was one more establishment to adjust to, but what heartened Elizabeth was that Dorothy Cockayne was able to visit her twice weekly to help her with her hobby. At that point she never dreamed that this 'hobby' would be the key to her independence.

# MOUTH PAINTING

Rosemary Howard clenched her teeth hard on the handle of a paint brush, leaned forward and attempted to apply colour to the board before her. Some of it reached the surface but what should have been a delicate line appeared as a long splodge which, though it might have delighted an action painter of the early sixties, brought a shudder to an elegant artist like herself.

'My God,' she murmured. 'How does she do it?'

The chain of events which led up to this experiment in her Walmer home had been initiated by a telephone call from Dr Boulden asking if she could give painting lessons to one of his patients. He explained that she was a quadraplegic who, having been shuttled between a variety of medical establishments, was once more with her parents at Mongeham.

Rosemary answered that, although she was an art teacher, she had no experience of instructing the disabled. But there was such a persuasive insistence in the doctor's voice that she heard herself agreeing to meet Miss Twistington Higgins to see if there was anything she could do.

Let us follow the story through Rosemary's own words:

'I rode out to the house on my bicycle and found her in the garden,' she relates. 'That day I just made contact. I looked at the rather elementary equipment she had, and she told me about her career as a dancer before she was paralysed. My first impression was of her tremendous determination to paint—I had never met anybody like her before. I noticed her hand on her lap and how her sister Alison gently put it back when it slipped. The fact that she did not have the ability to move it herself brought home to me that the most vital function an artist requires was, in her case, useless.

'Yet, because of her enthusiasm, I arranged to cycle over twice a week. She already had done some drawings with Miss Cockayne so I started to help her with colour mixing. It was a painfully slow process. To give you an idea, it took Elizabeth nine months to master the technique of loading a brush with paint. The problem is that she cannot move her head forward very far; the movement is sideways and up and down which gives her an effective paint area of only a few square inches. It is impossible for her to paint from one side of the board to the other, the board has to be moved into the orbit of her brush. At the time it was something she was unable to do herself.

'When I met her she was working on white paper with brown paint. That is one of the hardest things to do. To be faced with a blank piece of paper and put something down on it is very daunting. A great step forward was to get her to use coloured paper because if you have a coloured background there is something there already.

'At first our lessons were rather experimental. I had to lengthen her brushes in a way which did not make them too heavy, and we had to find out the best paper for taking paint easily. This had to be sized because oil paint turned out to be the best medium for her. We tried ink and watercolour, but this had to be abandoned because of its tendency to dribble downwards.

'Holding the brush in her mouth Elizabeth mixed the paint on a stationary palette. She had to have the colours put out for her, but she did the actual dipping and applying to the picture. We just cannot imagine what she must have gone through quite apart from the obvious physical difficulties. She would do a pleasing sketch and then — quite unexpectedly — jerk. The brush would slither down and all that effort would be wasted. Then we had to start again — or rather, she had to start again.

'My husband made her a special easel which had a sloping wooden block in front of it. This had holes in it, one of which held a little pot of turpentine to clean her brushes in, beside it was another with turpentine to thin the paint down.

'I set her painting groups of flowers because they are stationary but have plenty of colour. I used to look around my garden for interesting arrangements for her to paint, and she was so keen that she would work on after I left. But while she enjoyed painting flowers, it was always ballet pictures which were the main thing with her.'

In all Rosemary Howard taught Elizabeth for six years. The lessons at Mongeham soon came to an end as winter was approaching, with its threat of interrupted power supplies, and Elizabeth had to leave her parents' home once more. An artist himself, Dr Boulden was very sympathetic to her problem of accommodation. He saw that she needed to be somewhere within easy reach of her mother and father and somewhere congenial where she could persevere with her new-found interest. He approached the local Medical Officer of Health, a friendly Irishman named Dr Lynch, who suggested that she could stay in the Dover Isolation Hospital where she would receive all necessary medical care and be able to continue her art studies.

At the end of October Elizabeth — accompanied by her special type-writer, art equipment and breathing machine — arrived at the isolation hospital which stands on the hillside overlooking Dover. She found that it consisted of half a dozen cubicles, opening on to a verandah, each side of a central kitchen. Because there was not a lot of contagious disease in the area she sometimes had the use of the next cubicle as a studio, and what a joy it was. At nine o'clock each morning she was placed in her chair and painted solidly for two hours. The nurses were wonderfully helpful when it came to cleaning brushes and squeezing out paints.

*Rosemary Howard teaching Elizabeth at the Dover Isolation Hospital*

*'Elizabeth in Action' — a drawing by Sir William Russell Flint*

Work recommenced in the afternoon, with Rosemary continuing to visit her twice a week.

'She was desperately keen to paint ballet pictures,' Rosemary recalls. 'I made little cut-out figures to demonstrate anatomy. For example, an artist needs to know that a head goes into a body roughly seven times. And I helped her with perspectives, how figures would appear on stage when looked at from the circle.

'One of the difficulties she had to face was that, unlike artists who have the use of their hands, she could not make a preliminary sketch. Everything was straight down with the colour. Usually she started with the head and then put in the main lines, using very dry paint which gives a rather rough impression because it does not cover all the paper over which the brush passes. She would go over these lines and then put the dresses on.

'I found it very exciting when I saw her wonderful talent starting to develop. Often we lived through sloughs of despond together but I remember that she had a terrific sense of humour. Sometimes there would be hoots of laughter when things went wrong. When I left her I always thought, "Now I'm going home to my ordinary life, doing household chores and enjoying domestic things, but she's like that all day, every day." It preyed on my mind and at home I tried mouth painting myself so that I could understand what it felt like, but I was hopeless and I just gave up.

'We had to improve the equipment. The trouble was that she frequently bit through the wooden handles of the brushes. I tried binding on extra lengths of wood with twine but that did not help as it made the brush too heavy. Finally I used light plastic tubing with the brush handle stuck in one end. She still bit through the tube but it was replaceable. I encouraged her to use a big brush to get the big sweeping statements down. When she had to do detailed work with a small one she had to be careful because the lovely freedom of the big brush had gone.

'At the beginning I never guessed she would go so far as an artist; all I was concerned with was teaching her to paint so that she would have an interest in life. But as she progressed I saw that I was dealing with a real talent, especially when it came to her ballet pictures. She had a good sense of colour from the start, and I think her most inspired paintings are those of single figures. As a dancer she had all the right knowledge of how the body should go. A lot of people can do pretty dancing figures but they are not real ballerinas like Elizabeth's. Obviously inside herself she was dancing with those figures. When they were poised on one foot I felt she was somehow part of them; it was *her* arms that were extended and *she* was on the stage under the lights with those wonderful dancers grouped round her.

'It is terribly important for a teacher to know when to bow out. If you stay with your pupils too long you start them painting in the same style as yourself. The time came when I felt that Elizabeth had reached a point where she should develop on her own. One could no longer look upon her as a disabled person who could paint, she was an artist in her own right. This was brought home to me when I took one of her pictures to an East Kent Art Society exhibition. It was one of a spray of apple blossom which I had given her from my garden, and it was bought by someone who had no idea that it was the work of a mouth artist. So, I gradually began to ease myself out of teaching her, but it made me feel awful. I missed our sessions together so much.'

At Christmas, 1958, Elizabeth painted an arabesque figure in sepia which, although her father pronounced it very unanatomical, she decided to use as a Christmas card. A hundred copies of it were printed, one of which was sent to Kit who had helped her with her early attempts at painting. Not long afterwards Kit was interviewed about her charity work by Roy Nash, a reporter from the now-defunct *Star* newspaper. In the course of conversation she pointed to Elizabeth's card and he was so intrigued by it that she showed him the *Three Tomatoes on a Wedgwood blue plate*. Sensing a good story he wrote to the Dover Isolation Hospital authorities requesting permission to interview their resident painter.

The anticipated visit of a London journalist caused a lot of excitement among the staff and a lot of apprehension for Elizabeth. On the day he was expected Rosemary came early to display the paintings to their best advantage while the nurses took extra care with Elizabeth's hair. They even persuaded her to wear a little makeup for the occasion.

At two o'clock he arrived, a sturdy dark-haired man whose horn-rimmed glasses seemed to flash good humour to those about him. Elizabeth's nervousness of the Press melted before his charm and soon she was actually enjoying the interview. As a result the *Star* of April 16, 1959, carried a feature on her, part of which read:

'Two things impressed me tremendously about this young woman who smiled and joked in her wheelchair. One was her burning determination to overcome physical handicap, the other was the quality of her pictures — daffodils, frothy mimosa that looked good enough to pick. There were landscapes and a still life of apples and oranges that made you hungry for apples and oranges. But it is Elizabeth's studies of dancers that are so remarkable. When she was in *Song of Norway,* she posed in her dancing costume for that painter of lovely women — Sir William Russell Flint. He called the study *Elizabeth in Action.*

'"Now I'm going to send him one of my pictures and call it: *Elizabeth out of Action,"* laughed Elizabeth.

Roy Nash's article was the first public recognition of Elizabeth's talent, but another encouraging milestone was soon to come — her first one-person show.

'Gordon Busby, the Principal of the Dover School of Art, was terribly interested in Elizabeth and fixed up her first exhibition,' says Rosemary Howard. 'It was held in the foyer of the art school. I put the paintings on card mounts, Elizabeth paid to have them framed and they looked splendid. It was the first time she sold her work to the general public and you could see that it gave her a tremendous boost — she was on her way at last.'

An exhibition in the Dover Public Library followed, and interest in Elizabeth accelerated. That summer Jenny Poynting, who had been her night nurse at the National Hospital, visited her with her husband John Ripley. By a stroke of fortune John's printing company specialised in fine art reproduction and he selected three of her pictures to print as Christmas cards.

Meanwhile Roy Nash was busy on Elizabeth's behalf, proving that his interest had not been merely for the sake of a story, in fact he became one of her most indefatigable supporters. With a portfolio of her paintings under his arm he walked into the office of the Exhibitions Officer at the Royal Festival Hall in London. The result was that fifty of her pictures were displayed on coloured panels in the Queen's reception room during the Festival Ballet's Christmas season of *The Nutcracker.* Elizabeth was taken to London to see her work and found herself overawed by this grandiose setting.

Thanks to the Festival Hall exhibition one of her pictures was used as a cover for a medical magazine and the Medici Society later printed it as a

*Elizabeth at her first exhibition*

85

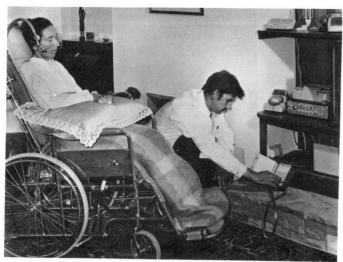

*Bob Blackburn testing equipment*

birthday card, the first of many of Elizabeth's paintings which the Society has reproduced as prints and greetings cards. The Cunard Line took two ballet designs which had been on display and used them as the covers of menus for their trans-Atlantic liners. Toc H asked Elizabeth to design their Christmas card and one of these duly reached their Patron, Queen Elizabeth the Queen Mother. Her Majesty sent a thoughtful letter of appreciation to the artist in the Dover Isolation Hospital.

\* \* \*

For two decades Elizabeth has been selling her work either as paintings which people buy at her exhibitions, or as artwork for prints and greetings cards. Looking at herself as a professional artist with an international reputation, she says, 'Joy in my work is always fleeting. Inevitably I soon detect faults and feel dissatisfied with my efforts. The more one learns of any of the arts, the more critical one becomes, and I have often ruined paintings by trying to improve them. Invariably my most successful pictures have been dashed off in carefree moments.

'It has taken twenty years to acquire the special painting equipment I have today. It has gradually evolved by a system of trial and error, and with the help of numerous inventive friends. Paint brushes have to be tailor-made to suit the individual artist — there can be no hard and fast rules. For myself as a mouth painter I find fourteen inches is a comfortable length for my eyesight. The handles are made of wood, which is very light and adapted to fit into ferrules which can be readily obtained. The mouth end must be waterproof to prevent the wood from rotting and tough enough to withstand a great deal of chewing.

'My electric easel is unique. It was designed so that the surface area for painting moves relative to my brush. This is necessary because I have very limited movement remaining in my neck. Left to my physical limitations I would only be able to paint an area of approximately four square inches.

'One of the biggest problems I still find in painting is that I can never keep the brush really steady. If I hold my breath to do a very fine line my heart starts to pound, which means that the heartbeats come out as a vibration on the end of the brush — sort of "heart throb" painting — so I can never do very fine work. I'm better with broader sweeps.

'I like to paint dancers, principally because this rids me of some of the desire to move. In spite of twenty-six years of immobility, I still long to dance again so I dance on paper. I also enjoy painting flowers, and I do a lot of Christmas cards, children playing in the snow or religious subjects such as Madonnas and angels — but in everything I feel there is movement.'

# CAMERA ANGLE

'Would you like to go to London for the weekend?' asked Matron in a strangely casual voice.

Propped up in a wheelchair in her 'studio' cubicle at the Dover Isolation Hospital, Elizabeth felt a pang of apprehension. Since she had become paralysed she seemed to have developed telepathic powers. Sometimes she would dream about somebody she had not thought of for years and the next day he or she would walk in on a surprise visit; often she knew exactly what she was going to be told before the person concerned had even opened his mouth.

'Why this weekend?' she asked.

'Oh well, the BBC... would like to interview... for *Town and Around...*

'Not *This is Your Life?*' Elizabeth asked with a flash of intuition. 'Oh no, I could never... No, no!'

The very idea of appearing on television provoked Elizabeth into an emotional outburst and her eyes filled with tears. Matron seemed understanding but disappointed at this unexpected reaction and leaving the room she said, 'Well, my dear, the decision is entirely up to you. Think it over and let me know what you decide in the morning.'

Rosemary Howard sighed. She knew that the rest of the afternoon was ruined as far as painting was concerned. She, too, had been in the know over the hush-hush BBC programme, and now she shared some of Matron's surprise at Elizabeth's reaction.

'I could not face my friends and relations saying kind and flattering things about me for half an hour,' explained Elizabeth. 'You know how kindness upsets me.'

'But I thought you stage people had a motto about the show always going on,' said Rosemary in calm and reasonable tones. 'Why, as a dancer you would have given anything to be on such a popular programme, to be seen by millions...'

And that was the subconscious obstacle. Elizabeth was no longer a dancer. In her last public performance at the London Coliseum she had been lithesome and lovely in a gorgeous costume. How could she

*One of Elizabeth's menu covers*

appear in a wheelchair after that? But Rosemary continued to appeal to her 'trouper' instinct by telling her that of three 'lives' prepared for the programme, two had left the country which only left her.

'If you don't appear they'll have to cancel the show,' she concluded with a telling psychological thrust.

The last thing Elizabeth could do was feel that she was letting other people down so reluctantly she decided to go through with it. Having sworn an oath of secrecy, she could not explain to the nurses what was making her so edgy.

On November 5, 1961, Elizabeth arrived at London's Middlesex Hospital and was admitted to the Observation Ward. The staff regarded her with curiosity. They sensed there was something out-of-the-ordinary about this case and their suspicions were confirmed early the following morning when a BBC team invaded her room for the recording of the *Town and Around* programme which was the official reason for her visit. Television cameras glided over the highly polished floor, technicians exchanged jokes in their private language, hot lights bathed the room in brilliant light then faded as the lighting man pondered a better angle. His earphones making him oblivious to the organised confusion about him, the sound man placed microphones and checked his levels.

At last a hush fell. The producer made a sign to Nancy Wise who opened the programme. When the interview came to the end Miss Wise said, 'As it is your birthday, Elizabeth, the BBC has prepared a surprise for you.' And right on cue Eamonn Andrews appeared and asked her with all his Irish charm if she would visit the television theatre that evening to see what else the BBC had in store for her.

Normally the first a subject knows about appearing on *This is Your Life* is when he suddenly finds himself in front of cameras but in this case it had been agreed with the medical authorities to give Elizabeth fair warning. A sudden shock could make her forget to breathe and the programme would find itself with more than its usual share of real-life drama. At the beginning of the programme Eamonn would explain that in this particular instance secrecy had been waived for medical reasons.

When the cameras and their snaking cables had been wheeled away Elizabeth was put into her respirator so she could rest during the afternoon. As dusk fell over wintery London nurses began preparing her for her ordeal and such was the rush that she missed seeing her interview on *Town and Around.*

The Resident Medical Officer appeared to give her a last-minute check-up before she was wheeled into a Daimler ambulance which arrived at Shepherd's Bush with only five minutes to spare. Luckily Elizabeth did not realise this because she has always had strict views on allowing plenty of time before a performance, and the seemingly-casual way television shows 'come together' at the very last moment is terrifying enough for the able-bodied let alone anyone who has to remember to take their every breath.

The ambulance reversed to a ramp and swiftly Elizabeth was wheeled on to a set where one of the boys she had danced with in *Song of Norway* placed a birthday gift on her lap—her first present that day. She only appreciated the thoughtfulness of the gesture when the show was over for as she was positioned by a table, on which pink carnations concealed microphones, she was only aware of the tense atmosphere around her.

'Everyone was willing me to give of my best,' she said later. Meanwhile she noticed a cylinder of oxygen in the wings—the BBC was not taking any chances. A make-up girl dusted her face lightly with powder; someone replaced the white pillowslip with blue. Beside her

*On television with Eamonn Andrews and her parents in 1961*

Eamonn chatted casually, and was still chatting when the theme music began.

Suddenly he was gone and Elizabeth heard his voice from the other side of the curtains.

'Tonight, *This is Your Life* is a birthday party,' he announced, 'with birthday surprises for one of the most remarkable and courageous young ladies I have ever met...'

The curtains swung back. Elizabeth saw a blur of faces in the auditorium and with a sudden shock, realised that she was on stage again.

The applause blended into music. Of course, what else but *Les Sylphides!* And on the monitor screens the audience saw a film recording of children dancing the Nocturne from this ballet. They were children from the Cone School where Elizabeth had once been both student and teacher, and they were the first to appear on the stage with her. After that successive periods of her life were brought into focus as Eamonn called out name after name and old friends walked into view. Jean Young, an Associate Member of the Royal Academy who had herself become a painter, talked about Elizabeth's dancing years; one of her best-ever pupils described what it was like to train under her, and so did Claire Bloom in a pre-recorded film from Hollywood.

Suddenly music from *Song of Norway* filled the auditorium, and on came John Hargreaves and Janet Hamilton-Smith to reminisce about the show and Elizabeth's part in it. They were soon joined by the choreographer Pauline Grant for whom she had so often danced. The Palace Theatre days were rounded off by anecdotes from the stage door-keeper Charles Reardon and memories of her panto days at the London Palladium were revived by the Bernard Brothers who appeared clowning as the Ugly Sisters.

Elizabeth had dreaded the programme, but as familiar faces appeared from her past she could have easily forgotten she was on television in the magic of those fleeting minutes, especially when she

'This is Your Life' *line-up*

saw the children she had taught at Coram's Fields smiling at her... Grimmer memories returned as Jenny Poynting talked about the long painful nights in the early days of her paralysis and Rosemary Howard described the terrible effort it had taken for her to become a mouth painter. Then Leslie Wilson of the Medici Galleries appeared just to say how successful that effort had been.

What could have been the thoughts of Tom and Jessie Twistington Higgins when they were ushered on and saw their paralysed daughter the centre of so much tribute and love? They were a reserved couple and seeing them in the bright stage light Elizabeth felt deeply sorry for them, knowing the strain it was for them to stand up in front of a theatre full of people — and fifteen million viewers — to say their carefully rehearsed lines.

From the Royal Ballet appeared Beryl Grey — who talked enthusiastically about Elizabeth's paintings — Margaret Roseby and David Blair, then Eamonn made traditional presentation of the script, the curtain fell... and then the real party began. Elizabeth was so exhausted she found it a great strain to chat to those who had come in secret to be with her for her big moment, but when she was finally wheeled back to the ambulance she would not have been surprised if it had turned into a pumpkin. To carry the analogy further, the Fairy Godmother role had been filled by Roy Nash of *The Star*. Believing that Elizabeth's work should receive wider exposure, he had written about it to the BBC *Monitor* art programme. His letter was passed to the 'appropriate department' which turned out to be *This is Your Life*.

Elizabeth was welcomed back to the Middlesex by the RMO who had watched her appearance on the screen with professional concern.

'I could tell how nervous you were at the start by the rapid movement of your neck muscles,' he said. 'It took ten minutes for your respiration rate to get back to normal.'

As a result of the programme the Dover Isolation Hospital received sackfuls of mail for Elizabeth. There were hundreds of letters to be answered and her family rallied to help her with the task. The bulk of them contained messages of goodwill or expressed thanks for the inspiration which Elizabeth's presence on the screen had brought.

A viewer in Worcester wrote typically: 'Thank you for appearing in *This is Your Life*. It is only by such a programme we realise what people like you achieve after what must, at first, seem the end to all activity. You must have helped many of us who are finding life in just its ordinary round rather difficult.'

A few of the letters were from cranks offering Elizabeth 'sure-fire' cures for her disability, the most innocuous one merely requiring that she take blackcurrant juice every half hour. Several letters were stranger still, suggesting that her failure to recover from paralysis was because she 'lacked faith'.

'Accepting a disability is an *act* of faith,' says Elizabeth, 'not a loss of faith. I have known other handicapped people who have received similar letters and been made utterly miserable by them.'

* * *

Although Elizabeth's physical condition remained constant, her inner life was changing. When she returned to Dover she was no longer a polio patient trying to re-establish herself with a paint brush; thanks to the BBC programme she had become a 'personality' in her own right. After the television broadcast there was such interest in her work that soon she had no more paintings to sell. Although she still remained in hospital and every night had to sleep in a breathing machine, it was a far cry from the days when she had lain listening to the 'swish-clunk' of the iron lung, tortured by the pointlessness of her life.

Certainly things had taken a turn that she could never have expected, but the old impossible dream remained — independence! Yet was it quite so impossible now? Though Elizabeth could see no way of becoming de-hospitalized, her few journeys to London by ambulance suggested that she could leave institutional life behind her for short periods. Why not an ambulance of her own?

At first the idea seemed too fraught with problems. She would like one in which she could travel in her wheelchair so she could enjoy the countryside, but how could a wheelchair be transferred into a vehicle with her already sitting in it? And there would be the question of a driver. But, helped by her father and some loyal friends in the Channel Islands, Elizabeth was able to persevere with her plan and a Folkestone company converted a Bedford Utilicon to her specifications. These included the raising of the roof to accommodate the wheelchair — held securely in place by special clamps — so that when she was reclining in it she could see out during the journey. For safety's sake she was to travel in this horizontal position because her neck is vulnerable to dislocation. So that the chair could be wheeled in and out of the vehicle Elizabeth designed special folding ramps which jack-knifed into position. In case of emergency the private ambulance carried a cylinder of oxygen and later a positive pressure machine with a heavy duty battery to power it. The cost of these modifications turned out to be more than the price of the Utilicon, but on the brighter side Elizabeth found that there were always drivers willing to chauffeur her.

Members of the Deal Ambulance Service drove her with comforting professionalism in their spare time.

Having her own transport after nine years of being restricted to hospital was a symbol of independence which, instead of satisfying Elizabeth, strengthened a growing resolve to lead a more normal life — and this could only be done by somehow achieving a home of her own.

*Elizabeth's first personal ambulance — a converted Bedford Utilicon*

*Elizabeth's father squeezing her paints in Kent, 1958*

# COMMERCIAL ARTIST

For the background to the next development in Elizabeth's life we should consider Arnulf Erich Stegmann. Born sixty-seven years ago in Darmstadt he was crippled by poliomyelitis at the age of three. His hands and arms were to remain without use and his legs were affected to a lesser degree. Unable to behave like normal children, there emerged out of his humiliation a terrible resolve to earn a great deal of money as he saw it as the only means by which to win independence for himself.

At school he tried to surpass his able-bodied fellow pupils, especially in the field of art for which he had a vocation. They seemed to be able to paint and draw so effortlessly with pens or brushes in their fingers while he toiled to get the same results with a brush held in his mouth.

But so successful was he with this novel technique that at fifteen he was allowed to enrol at a prestigious art school. Five years later his first painting was hung at the famous Nuremburg Gallery Novis and the Albrecht-Durer Foundation granted him a scholarship to spend a year in the studio of the Hungarian painter Erwin von Kormendy. By the age of twenty-two he was independent enough to leave home and share a studio with his brother-in-law in Munich. With the rise of the Nazi Party someone as devoted to the cause of individual independence as Stegmann inevitably found himself in trouble, and in December, 1934, he was arrested as 'an enemy of the Nazi State'.

It is hard to imagine the horror of being in prison without the use of one's hands, and as a final refinement of cruelty he was not permitted to have his art materials. After fifteen months in captivity a police doctor declared him unfit to remain a prisoner and, as there was no evidence to bring him before a judge, he was released in March, 1936. But the threat of the Gestapo remained hanging over him and as a result of his continued opposition to the regime he had to spend the latter part of the war in hiding away from his home.

In 1932 he had started his own publishing house and as a businessman he has fulfilled his early dream of making enough money to afford the 'luxury' of a self-determined life. As an artist he has exhibited from Jerusalem to Sydney, from Tokyo to London, and he has been the recipient of numerous awards for his creative work. These include the *Officer de Pordre du merite Paris 1971* and the exotic-sounding *Ehrenmitglied der Accademia artis templum sassari 1968*.

Professor A.E.Stegmann

What is remarkable about his artistic output is its wide range — pencil drawing, oil painting and watercolour; lino and wood-cuts made with the stylo clamped between his teeth and, most surprising of all, woodcarving. In her book *When One Door Closes...* Eileen Waugh wrote of him, 'He can, and does, paint in numerous styles, each expressing a different side of his nature. There are his paintings of children, his gentle paintings, his violent and aggressive paintings, his paintings with a sociological message, his paintings in the style of the old masters; each is outstanding in its own way...'

Having achieved his personal goal this tough-looking, flaxen-haired painter, with his powerful torso and atrophied arms, wondered about the plight of other handicapped artists. In 1947 he began seeking them out all over the world and then set up the Association of Mouth and Foot Painting Artists with its headquarters in Liechtenstein.

For over thirty years he has travelled from country to country on behalf of its members, organising exhibitions of their work and supervising the sale of greetings cards and calendars specially painted for reproduction. Two hundred different designs are produced each year. The profit from this massive international undertaking goes to provide each member of the Association with a generous monthly salary. Once a disabled artist has been accepted into the Association he or she will receive that salary for life even if a worsening physical condition puts an end to their artistic output. There is also an annual bonus for those artists who produce extra work for the benefit of the Association. The effect of this regular money on handicapped painters is hard for healthy people to appreciate. Psychologically it provides a necessary sense of security; in practical terms it means an end to financial anxiety, it makes possible the hiring of helpers to enable them to live outside institutions, and it ensures that all are free to concentrate on their painfully-gained creativity.

No candidate is accepted for membership until an independent board has examined his or her work and pronounced it of sufficiently high standard to compare favourably with that of able-bodied professional artists. Often young handicapped people who show promise are given training by the Association to bring them up to a standard which will make them eligible for membership.

Following the *This is Your Life* programme Elizabeth was approached to join the Association.

'It took me a long time to decide whether or not to join,' Elizabeth explains. 'The contract was so good it seemed fishy. For example, I was told that I would receive my salary for life whether or not I could continue painting, and they would even continue to pay my relatives for three months after I "passed on" because they would still be getting the benefit of my work. It all sounded too good to be true and I showered questions on Mr Heinz, who looks after the British side of the Association, but he always gave me reasonable answers and it began to appear I could not go wrong by joining. However, I did not want to abandon the contacts I had already made on my own in the art world, and there were long discussions about my contract as it meant the Association would have the monopoly of my work. Eventually, it was agreed that some of my work could be used by other firms but they could not mention that it was painted by mouth and the Association had to be kept informed.

'Since signing my contract I have never regretted my decision. It was the beginning of a more independent existence for me and it is greatly to the credit of Eric Stegmann — our President — that we disabled artists throughout the world can have real security.

'Yet, almost unbelievably, I found that security itself can take some of the zest out of work. Under the contract I could sit back for three or four months and do nothing and still get paid. I suppose the most exciting work is that which is not commissioned, when you have no idea what the reaction to it will be. And the work I have always enjoyed doing most I have done for nothing, such as my charity work.

'Not that this security holds me back. I supply the Association with at least a dozen paintings each year. Some are sold in exhibitions around the world, and an average of five are published annually as cards and calendars which is a very high percentage when you remember there are over fifty full members of the Association.

'Since I have joined nearly a hundred of my paintings have been published and the sales of many of them have run into millions. I have had letters of appreciation from all over the world, some from nurses who cared for me in the early stages of my illness and who had now returned to their homes in America, Australia, Canada and New Zealand. This could not have been achieved without the assistance of the nursing staff at the isolation hospital and members of the Dover Red Cross who came regularly to help me.'

One matter regarding the Association which made Elizabeth indignant was the publication a couple of years ago of a newspaper article which suggested that the disabled members of the Association were being exploited.

'Another member rang me up and warned me that a reporter — complete with hidden microphone in his pocket — would soon be knocking on my door,' Elizabeth says. 'The member's suspicions had been aroused by the nature of the leading questions he had asked. In fact the reporter rang up and asked whether I would agree to be interviewed. I said no, and that anyway I had already given a lot of interviews, so he tried questioning me over the telephone. These were exactly the questions I had been warned about, and it was obvious that he was trying to make out a case that we were being exploited by the Association — *which was ridiculous because we are the Association.*

'When I saw the article in print I was absolutely disgusted. It was so wrong I could hardly believe it. I wrote a reply, as did the other British artists but not one line of apology ever appeared in the newspaper. To them the suggestion that something as respectable as the Association was cheating handicapped people made a good sensational story, but the effect it had was despicable.

'We are not exploited. If anything we are overpaid for what we do.'

Among Elizabeth's friends in the Mouth and Foot Painting Artists are those whose experiences have proved that, like her, disability can be overcome by a combination of determination and co-operation. Peter Spencer, MBE, lost the use of his arms in an accident in 1945 while he was serving as an RAF pilot. After he began to paint by holding a brush in his mouth he recieved an MFPA scholarship which enabled him to enter the Wallasey College of Art, of which he is now a Governor. As a successful painter he has been able to lead an independent life, he is married with two children and drives a converted Mini controlled entirely by his feet. Appropriately he is now the appointed Trustee for the MFPA Fund for the Training of Handicapped Children in Arts and Crafts.

Charles Fowler lost both arms in a railway accident at the age of eighteen, yet he continued his art career with a brush clamped between his teeth, with the result that his work was exhibited at the Royal Academy. Later he became Head of the Art Department at Richmond Adult College. Like his colleagues in the MFPA he has refused to let disability hamper him and he frequently lectures on behalf of the partnership.

An artist who paints with his foot is Paul Driver, who specializes in marine scenes, landscapes and flowers. A victim of poliomyelitis, he had to spend a year in an iron lung and now — like Elizabeth — he still has to sleep in a respirator.

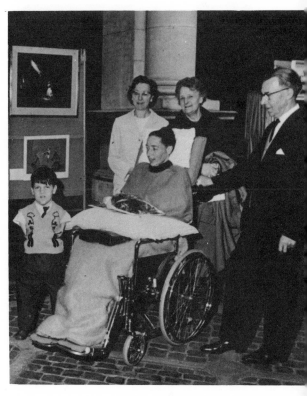

*Elizabeth at the Mouth and Foot Painting Artists Exhibition with Johnnie, Janet Harvey, Jane and Bill Roos*

Such is the spirit of Elizabeth's colleagues. In other times society would have written them off, but by their own efforts, channelled through their partnership, they are self-supporting artists who have given pleasure to millions through reproductions of their work.

Other mouth painters include Albert Baker who, despite numerous surgical operations, has very limited use of his hands, arms and legs, yet he struggled to become an artist and now gains inspiration through the lovely Hampshire countryside for his essentially English landscapes which have been exhibited around the world.

The first thing that a regular income meant to Elizabeth was the possibility of a specially adapted home where she could lead her own life away from hospital routine, and a long search began for a suitable house or flat. The months dragged by but nothing fulfilling her exacting requirements came on the market.

One dreary winter's day in 1964 she was beginning to wonder if she would ever find the home she was seeking. The splashing of the raindrops on the large window of the cubicle and the dark low-flying clouds racing in from the Channel, made a sombre setting for her thoughts. Oh! To see the sun again! To feel its warmth and watch blue waves turning to white foam on golden beaches!

Without much interest Elizabeth put the rubber ferrule of her mouth stick against a page of the *Radio Times* and turned it to find herself looking at an enticing advertisement for a Cunard cruise.

The thought was preposterous... *but why not* make some enquiries?

When Dr Lynch did his round that afternoon, she asked.

'Do you think I could go on a cruise?'

He laughed good-humouredly, he was used to Elizabeth's jokes.

'I'm serious,' she said.

'I see no reason why you shouldn't,' he declared. 'There's plenty of electricity on board ship, and come to think of it, with the threat of winter power cuts here, you may well be *safer* at sea.'

So it was decided that Elizabeth should have a three-week Mediterranean cruise — if Cunard would agree. A letter was sent to the company

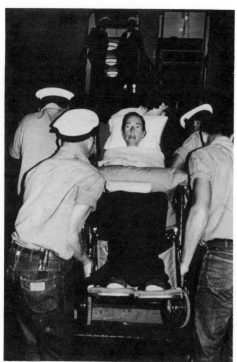
*Being lifted aboard the 'R.M.S. Mauretania' in 1964*

parents who had decided to accompany her. Two respirators should be taken, both working from the ship's electrical supply; a Beaverometer operated by a twelve volt battery, and spare parts for all three machines. She promised not to drink or eat local food when ashore. Her T.A.B. would be waived... and so on.

As part of the extraordinary thoroughness which was the keynote of the operation, the exact measurements and photographs of Elizabeth's wheelchair were sent to the *Mauretania* and to the International Red Cross which was arranging transport at each port of call. The biggest obstacle was Elizabeth's passport because she was unable to sign it. In the end the Commandant of the Dover Red Cross Society travelled to London to arrange a dispensation for her.

Although the *Mauretania* carried three nurses aboard, it was decided it would be best for Elizabeth to take her own helpers. Her sister Alison and Janet Harvey, a friend who was an SRN, volunteered to go. Early one drizzling morning the party arrived by the towering, pale green side of the *Mauretania* at Southampton and found Dr Heggie there to welcome Elizabeth aboard and to introduce her to the ship's Medical Officer. A lift took her up to A deck where the company had thoughtfully placed her and her family in a large suite at the centre of the ship where they would be least affected by rough weather.

Elizabeth remembers that her cabin was like a florist's shop with *bon voyage* bouquets. A seemingly endless stream of people was introduced to her, including Cunard shore staff who had helped make the unique holiday possible and specialist members of the crew who would be looking after her during it.

From her wheelchair on the sun deck she watched the shoreline of the Solent slip past as the great liner headed for the sea. Returning to her cabin she was reassured to find several of the ship's engineers looking over the motors of her breathing equipment so they would know what to do in case of breakdown. That night the ship started to roll as it encountered a gale but, though many of the passengers were seasick, Elizabeth felt no ill effects — the motion was similar to the rocking bed she had once endured.

When the *Mauretania* reached Tangier she wondered how Captain Treasure Jones would keep his promise to get her ashore while the ship was anchored in the bay. She found out when she and her family reached the main deck and four sturdy sailors lifted her, chair and all, into the ship's launch. When the rest of the party was seated, crisp orders were given and the launch was swung out on its davits and lowered to the sea which seemed so far below. It was the same procedure as for abandoning ship.

After Elizabeth had enjoyed her first day's sight-seeing on North African soil the launch arrived at the quay to take her back and the operation was reversed with the boat being hoisted up on the davits.

A rough sea cancelled a visit to Valetta, and Elizabeth innocently asked Captain Treasure Jones if it would be possible to visit Malta on the way back.

'I can't promise, m'dear,' he replied, 'but I'll radio London and see what can be done.'

She thought that he was saying this just to please her but later she found out he did obtain permission to travel two hundred miles off course so that she should not be disappointed.

The *Mauretania* reached Alexandria on April 1 and a delegation from the Egyptian Red Crescent came aboard to welcome Elizabeth, and soon afterwards a convoy of vehicles took her and her family on a three-day marathon of sight-seeing during which she was presented with

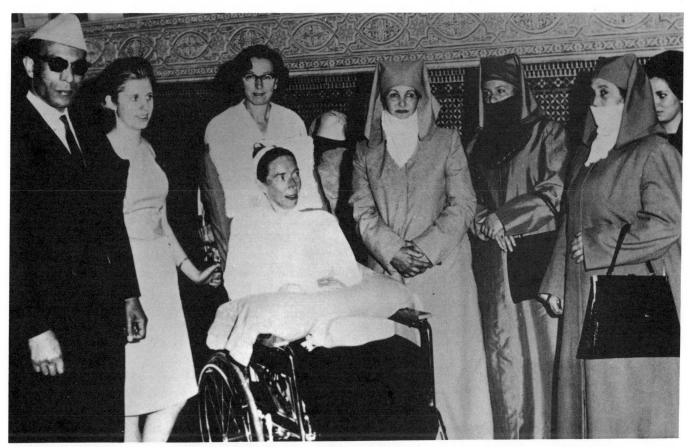

*Reception at the Sultan's Palace with members of the Moroccan Red Crescent*

flowers on every possible occasion. The newspapers were full of photographs and articles on the visit though what the journalists said about her remained a mystery as she could not read Arabic.

From Egypt the liner swung northwards to Greece where an old friend was waiting to greet Elizabeth. She was one of the doctors who had escorted her on her first outing to Covent Garden and was now living with her husband and family in Athens. Thanks to her efforts Elizabeth was to be the guest of the Greek Red Cross who continued the tradition of care and hospitality established by the Red Crescent. The high point of the visit, in more ways than one, was when the party arrived at the Acropolis and Elizabeth was physically carried up the steep slope to the Parthenon.

'Large boulders were strewn on the ground all around and it was impossible to find enough level ground on which to rest the chair,' she wrote later. 'It was certainly an endurance test for my kindly porters, but they gave me one of the most memorable mornings of my life.'

As those who have visited the Parthenon know it is a moving experience to stand under colonnades dating back five centuries before the birth of Christ, and look over the city to legendary Mount Hymettus rising against a backdrop of lustrous blue. It was the most magical moment of Elizabeth's magical journey, for nothing symbolised her escape from years of physical restriction more than this panorama of the ancient world.

*At the traditional Captain's Party with Captain Treasure Jones*

Next came Malta, thanks to the captain taking her wish seriously, and here she was entertained at the Governor's Residence. An invitation had also been sent to Sir Henry Seddon who was visiting the island, and who had been Elizabeth's specialist at the Royal National Orthopaedic Hospital at Stanmore nine years previously.

'We could meet in England, Elizabeth,' he said, running his professional eye over her. 'We shouldn't need to come all this way.'

At Gibraltar the Red Cross had organised a Royal Naval patrol car with

*In Israel the Star of David lends this ambulance*

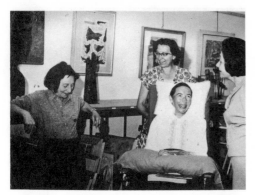

*Talking to Gertrude Krauz — Israel's leading choreographer turned painter — with Janet Harvey in the centre.*

a couple of military policemen to show Elizabeth the sights.

'Makes a nice change from picking up drunken sailors,' said one cheerfully.

The next day the ship sailed up the Tagus to dock at Lisbon where the Portuguese Red Cross had gone one better — they had provided a bullfighter as a chauffeur.

The end of every voyage has its moment of sadness; brief friendships come to an end, a pattern of living is suddenly no more and the holiday atmosphere wilts as everyday realities take over. For three weeks Elizabeth had enjoyed more new experiences, more colour and adventure, than she had known during the eleven years she had been disabled. Now as her ambulance took her back to the Dover Isolation Hospital, her kaleidoscope of memories was strengthening her resolve to do it again someday. Among her souvenirs lay a token of what others had felt about her enterprise. It was a white sailor's cap which had arrived mysteriously in her cabin and had been autographed by the *Mauretania's* bosun and many members of the crew.

At Dover it was back to work with a vengeance, preparing paintings for an exhibition at which she was to receive the ultimate tribute to an artist — someone liked one of her paintings enough to steal it by cutting it from the wall.

Later on Elizabeth booked on the *Mauretania's* last cruise. This time she landed at Haifa where representatives of the Star of David (the Red Cross of Israel) took her to the art colony of Ein Hod. Here she was given a heart-warming reception by artists who already knew her work because of the huge number of her greeting cards which had been sold in Israel. Among those welcoming her was Gertrude Krause, the country's leading choreographer who, like Elizabeth, had channelled her talent into painting.

When the *Mauretania* finally docked at Southampton the end-of-the-cruise feeling was more noticeable than usual because both passengers and crew were aware that the ship's next voyage would be to the breaker's yard. But for Elizabeth the return was one of high hope rather than regret — just before the cruise her father had located a ground-floor flat in Walmer which sounded ideal. And so it turned out to be. Within forty-eight hours he had helped her to buy it and now, on her return to England, she would be setting up a home of her own.

*Malcolm Salmon at control console*

# MECHANICAL LIZ

It is hard for those with no experience of disability to imagine the elation which Elizabeth felt one August day in 1965 when her ambulance drove up to a sea-front flat in Walmer and she was wheeled into her own home. For twelve years home had been a small area of hospital floorspace but now—thanks to her earnings as an artist—she was moving into a place that was truly hers. Of course at night-time she would have to return to the Dover Isolation Hospital to sleep in a breathing machine, but each whole day would be hers. She felt that the impossible had been achieved; despite all the odds she had gained independence from institutionalization.

It is the human condition that no emotion can last be it intense happiness or deep despair, but some experiences are so deep they remain vivid in memory no matter what other experiences overlay them. So that golden day on which Elizabeth began her new life will always be fresh in her mind—not only did it signify a triumph over disability but also over bureaucracy and prejudice.

Her father had tried to convince the Minister of Health and other officials that, given sufficient help, severely disabled respiratory cases could live out of hospital. The results of his efforts were most discouraging and, in the light of what has since been achieved, the replies to his letters now seem positively archaic. In desperation he decided to go it alone and set about finding somewhere near the hospital where his daughter could lead a more normal life.

But he and Elizabeth were in for some shocks. The leasing of one flat was refused on the grounds that it would not be *nice* for the other tenants in the block—it would be turning the building into a nursing home.

'The place for your daughter is in hospital,' this brilliant surgeon was told, 'and the sooner she comes to terms with herself and accepts this, the happier she will be.'

When Elizabeth heard this she was appalled.

She thought she had come to terms with disability, but she had not resigned herself to a life sentence in an institution. Certainly she was immobile, certainly she was dependent upon a machine, but she was normal in every other respect including the desire to live in her own home.

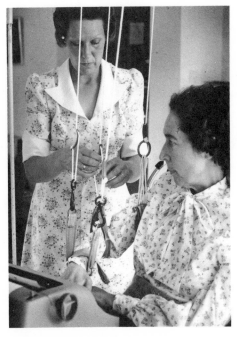

*Averil Brown setting Elizabeth to type*

*Elizabeth with POSM control*

When a suitable flat was finally found her father told her, 'I ought to warn you that one or two of the people living there have been raising objections about having a disabled person as a neighbour.'

Recalling that period, Elizabeth says, 'When I'd been there for a while they all admitted that they had written a "round robin" letter to the owners of the flats to say that they didn't think that I would be a suitable neighbour. I think they thought I wouldn't be as clean as themselves, but, when they got to know me, they found that my flat was probably cleaner than theirs — thanks to my helpers! I think that the problem arose because I had come from the Infectious Diseases Hospital, they were afraid that I was going to bring something "nasty" with me. They just didn't understand. I think people are prejudiced against disablement. When I got to know them better, they had admitted that they had been quite wrong, and in the end they became very good neighbours to me — all of them.'

Once the flat had been bought an architect was engaged to supervise necessary innovations. These included fitting strong beams across the bathroom and bedroom ceilings to which were attached rail tracks. These supported a sliding hoist with nylon slings tailored to fit Elizabeth's body so she could be lifted and moved by one helper.

It was on the question of helpers that Elizabeth's plans nearly foundered. At first she and her mother tried to find someone who would live in, but they were disappointed to find that the applicants' only interest seemed to be in a home for themselves and not in the work. In the end it was decided to have a rota of part-timers — paid at the same rate as hospital auxiliaries — and the system has worked admirably to this day.

The twice-daily journeys were to prove too difficult for Elizabeth's ambulance drivers to fit in with their professional driving duties. She was put in touch with the WVS who, as though by magic, arranged a rota of four jolly Trinity House Pilots to drive her voluntarily on the days when they were not employed guiding ships in the Channel. Although they had had no previous contact with disabled people they looked after Elizabeth with such good-humoured competence that she soon felt completely confident in their care, and she never missed a day at home for the want of a driver.

Not all relationships with those who were involved in her welfare were quite so cheerful. On one occasion she went to her parents' home for a few days which meant visits from the district nurse. When this lady pulled down the bedclothes for the first time she gazed at Elizabeth in horror — never having seen anyone so disabled before — and muttered, 'This is the Devil's own handiwork.' Then looking at the respirator, she inquired, 'How long d'you think you'll have to be in this?'

'Oh, for the rest of my life,' replied Elizabeth lightly.

'Well, dear, one good thing,' said the nurse, 'people like you don't live very long.'

\* \* \*

Apart from her human helpers Elizabeth's new found independence was to depend upon an amazing piece of electronic equipment known as POSM — the initials standing for 'Patient Operated Selector Mechanism'. It is also known appropriately as Possum, the Latin for 'I am able'.

One of the medical stipulations was that if Elizabeth was to spend her days in her own flat she should be able to use a telephone in case of emergency. Until the advent of 'Possum' such an idea would have been unthinkable, but in the mid-Sixties a brilliant inventor named Reg

Maling, and his assistant, Roger Jefcoate, demonstrated equipment they had pioneered to doctors and physiotherapists at the National Hospital for Nervous Diseases. As the two put their gadgetry through its paces Matron commented, 'Of course, we are all thinking of the same person to whom it would be useful.' And so the Possum research team visited Elizabeth's flat and installed the equipment.Today, it is the Possum Environmental Control which makes Elizabeth's life at Chelmsford possible.

Mounted on her wheelchair, within easy reach of her mouth, is a slender plastic tube. By sucking or blowing into it she can activate the electronic unit to perform a number of necessary functions. It enables her to summon her helper, speak to people when they press the door-bell, open the front door by means of an electrical device, and control the radio, television, lighting, heating and electric fan. Also by sucking and blowing a dictation machine and tape-recorder can be operated, as can an external alarm bell in case of an emergency such as a fire. A double row of illuminated panels indicates whichever function the equipment is set to, while a row of red numbers from one to zero is used for 'dialling' a telephone call. A series of puffs moves a light along these numbers until the required digit is illuminated, the patient then blows until the moving light reaches the next one, and so on.

The telephone apparatus itself is a combination of Possum ingenuity and a Post Office LST5B, or loudspeaker phone, for which Elizabeth has to pay a considerably higher rental than for a usual telephone installation. Such is the sophistication of the equipment that if she is on the telephone and suddenly needs to use another Possum facility — for example, someone arrives at the front door and needs to be admitted — she merely has to 'dial' 4-0 to be able to make her selection without ringing off.

The importance of these electronic aids to Elizabeth's way of life cannot be over-stressed and later we shall see the vital role they played in making what seemed the utterly impossible come about. She is very aware of what they have meant to her and her disabled colleagues and in the magazine *Responant,* published for the severely disabled, she wrote: 'Machines, in fact, are such a vital part of US now that we cannot live without them, and I mean "live" in the widest sense of the word. Machines today are enabling totally paralysed people to achieve the seemingly impossible. But behind all these machines are people: inventors, manufacturers, engineers, electricians, doctors, helpers and many others — people who labour unceasingly to enrich our lives. We are fortunate to be living in this era when so much is done for us and when the future promises even more.'

\* \* \*

One of the great pleasures of Elizabeth's new flat was that at last all her possessions were assembled together again. For over twelve years they had been stored with different members of the family but now treasured pieces of furniture were once more in place, familiar pictures hung on the walls and there were the rows of old books and a pile of records. Although the flat was new to her, her arrival was in a sense a home-coming.

The other great joy of the flat was its situation overlooking the Goodwin Sands — at low tide gold and inviting but a notorious shipping hazard — and The Downs where vessels shelter during Channel storms. Elizabeth had only to glance out of her window to see the busiest shipping lane in the world; there were always huge tankers and passenger liners outlined on the horizon, closer to land cargo carriers set their courses on the trade routes of North Europe while inshore bobbed fishing boats and the colourful triangles of the local yacht club.

*Reg Maling, inventor of Possum*

*Left— Evensong about to start.
Elizabeth is welcomed by Father Stroud*

It was an ideal setting for an artist and Elizabeth took full advantage of it. Her reputation as a painter had been made at the Dover Isolation Hospital, but no matter how encouraging its staff were she could never quite rid herself of the fear she might be asking too much of the girls whose duty it was to nurse rather than squeeze out tubes of paint. Here she need not have such qualms.

One darkening cloud hung over Elizabeth, her father was ailing and had to spend much of his time in bed which was highly tedious for someone who had lived an energetic life.* In July, 1966, this remarkable man died and Elizabeth lost her most constant supporter. He had done everything he could for her from every standpoint, but perhaps the most important of all was to impress upon his daughter that though she was disabled she was still a person in her own right.

Dame Ninette de Valois once described how one afternoon she was sitting with Elizabeth in her flat in Walmer.

'Suddenly I was made acutely aware of a great force in her life — her father,' she said. 'It was a chance remark on Elizabeth's part, but for me a curtain parted, letting in a flood of light.'

Elizabeth later wrote: 'My illness had caused my father much anxiety and when his prayers for my recovery were answered, I was told that he suffered agonies of doubt as to whether he had asked too much of God. When I started to paint, however, his doubts were swept away. "This," he said, "is the miracle I have waited for," and he was able to rejoice with me in my new-found career.'

Following the shock of his death Elizabeth found it impossible to paint for many dreary weeks. Everything was there; the tubes of paint, the willing helpers, the right ambience — all that was missing was the motivation.

It was pure professionalism which made her take her brush holder between her teeth again. Christmas was approaching and there were unfulfilled orders for greeting card designs. Because she could not let her publishers down she started painting again, working twice as hard as normal to catch up with the backlog of work. The result was that her neck muscles — without which she could not breathe when out of a respirator — became over-taxed. To her dismay she began to lose control of her brush. It would twitch infuriatingly when it was supposed to make a straight line. Daily it got worse. It was as though the agonising process of learning to mouth paint was reversed and she was returning to square one.

She was X-rayed. Mercifully there was no bone damage, but the orthopaedic specialist forbade painting and ordered a long course of physiotherapy to relieve the muscular strain.

After a few weeks of treatment the pain began to lessen, but when she experimented with a brush paint splattered over the paper as it twitched out of control.

A terrible fear grew within her. She had already lost one career when she was at her peak — was her career as an artist to end like her dancing career fourteen years earlier? But if she had lost her painting technique, her creativity remained unquenched, and she sought another outlet for it. With her arm slung below an overhead frame she began to tap out a book on her electric typewriter.

'To prevent myself from thinking too much about the disappointment, I started putting down my experiences,' she wrote. 'For years the idea had hovered in the back of my mind and I had made one or two tentative starts. With the suspension of my artistic pursuits, it seemed that

*Thomas Twistington Higgins*

*While this book was being written Elizabeth discovered that as a youth he had to make the choice between playing professionally for Manchester United and going to medical school.

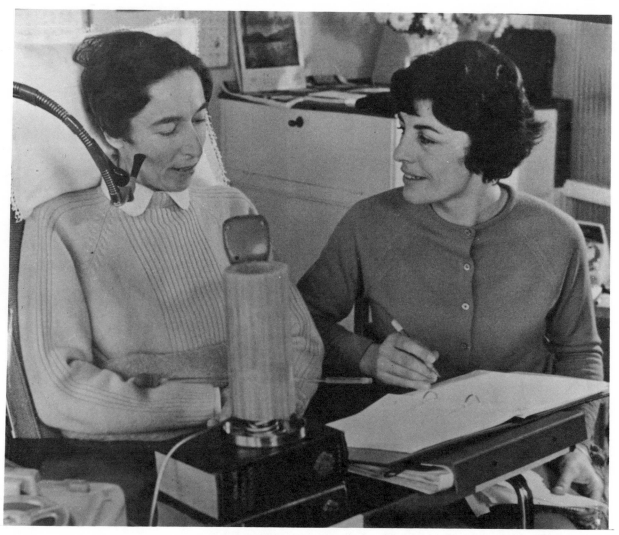

*Working on "Still Life" with secretary Jacqueline Basford*

Providence was directing me to get on with it. Inspiration invariably came in the middle of the night when I was not distracted with thoughts of breathing and had uninterrupted peace and quiet. I had no means of recording these ideas though, and often failed to recapture them in the morning. It was a tremendously stimulating challenge, however, and I enjoyed creating in a new medium.'

With secretarial assistance from Jacqueline Basford the book was completed and, under the title of *Still Life,* it was published in 1969, and was later translated into seven languages. It so impressed Godfrey Winn that he proclaimed Elizabeth as his 'Woman of the Year'.

\* \* \*

At the end of 1968 family circumstances made it necessary for Elizabeth to leave her beloved flat. Her mother was ageing and understandably missing her husband, and it was decided that she should not live alone. Plans were made for her to stay with her daughter Janet, but she would only settle in a new home if she knew Elizabeth was within easy reach of a member of the family once she had left Kent.

Elizabeth's sister Brighid, who lived in Chelmsford, found her an attractive house on the outskirts of the town, and nearby Broomfield Hospital agreed to take her as a regular over-night patient. By November Elizabeth's flat had been sold and she was faced with the ordeal of moving. It was a wrench to be taking leave of her helpers whom she had come to know and trust, and to say goodbye to the staff of the Dover Islolation Hospital where she had been for twelve years. The anticipation of setting up a new home was appalling. Changing house for the physically fit is always a strain, for someone as paralysed as Elizabeth it can be horrendous. Apart from the necessity of having her new home adapted to her needs, she faced the prospect of getting used to the nightly routine of a new hospital, and of engaging a completely new team of helpers and drivers.

It was heart-breaking as she watched her flat being dismantled, her helpers supervising the removal of her furniture to Chelmsford. Then with Ron, who had driven her for eight years, she left in her ambulance followed by a van containing her respirators and Possum equipment from the isolation hospital.

Broomfield Hospital is an old tuberculosis sanitorium set in lovely surroundings. As Elizabeth was wheeled into Ward 1 she found it to be made up of single and double cubicles opening on to a wide, airy corridor which seemed to stretch to infinity.

She was placed in Room 6 which had been thoughtfully decorated in the same pink shade as her room at the Dover Isolation Hospital. One wall was made up of a folding glass door which gave her a splendid view over a garden without another building in sight. As her equipment was carried in she felt an old embarrassment, there was such a lot of apparatus required to keep her alive and soon the room was filled and it overflowed into the corridor. Memories of past complaints that she made the ward untidy returned but the sister of Ward 1 was no martinet. Understanding how the new patient felt, she made light of it and there was universal laughter after lunch when the Possum Research team arrived to set up their specialised apparatus and reported that their greeting at the hospital entrance had been, 'What are you then, Pest Control?'

The next day Elizabeth was taken to her house where the GPO had already installed her telephone system. A large room, looking out on a pleasant garden with fruit trees, made an ideal studio. Here she began interviewing ladies who had replied to Brighid's advertisements for helpers. Two of the applicants proved to be both charming and willing which meant that she would be able to start her domestic routine within a few days though of course she needed more.

Today she has a rota of ten, some of whom have been with her since her arrival in Chelmsford. To find such devoted people was not easy and she had to continue the exhausting task of interviewing and explaining her needs and routine — exhausting because while going over the same ground again and again she had to fit her sentences round her breathing pattern.

'When I do get the right people they're really wonderful,' she says. 'They *are* my *human* life support system. If I couldn't rely on their constant and generous help, the wheels would grind to a halt and I should be utterly helpless. But to find them is difficult. When I was recruiting my team I advertised in the local newspaper. As a result Cecilia phoned and when I explained that I was paralysed from the neck down she said, "Oh, could you call round and see me? I live in a cottage in Plum Lane."

'I should have seen the light then, but I was desperate for help. "No, I can't," I said. "I'm in a wheelchair."

'"Oh, shall I come round and see you then?" We made an appointment and when she arrived I asked the usual questions and she replied "Yes" to everything. Beggars can't be choosers, so I asked her to come in the next afternoon to try the job. She arrived late and plonked herself down in the armchair. My heart sank, I just knew she wasn't going to be any good. My helper Hannah had been looking after me all morning, and she was obviously vastly amused by this behaviour. Controlling her desire to laugh, she asked casually, "Shall I show you how to lower the wheelchair

*Rosemary Howard presenting Elizabeth with a bouquet*

105

to get Elizabeth into a resting position?"

"If you want to," replied Cecilia.

'Hannah demonstrated the various knobs and levers, but it was obvious that she was not taking in a single thing. Then with some trepidation Hannah had to leave me in the hands of this moron to go and collect her children from school.

'I had a nightmare afternoon with Cecilia. Even the simplest of jobs seemed to be beyond her. In spite of Hannah's most careful instructions, she hadn't a clue how to manipulate the chair. At one stage she had me hanging half out of it and then proceeded to have hysterics, yelling, "I can't do it! I can't do it!"

'The cure for hysterics is a slap on the face, but how on earth could I do that? Instead, I put on my evenest tone of voice and said, "Cecilia, there is no one else in the house, you have GOT to do it. Now just do what I say." I hoped my words didn't betray my fear. Slowly I was re-installed in an upright position in my chair.'

This anecdote illustrates more than anything Elizabeth's dependence upon helpers and to find herself in the hands of someone who panicked was a nightmare situation. A slight fall means little to us, usually a hand can be put out to lighten it. In Elizabeth's case she would crash like an inanimate object and her bones, brittle after years of paralysis, would probably snap on impact. If she was knocked unconcious death would come quickly as breathing is only possible when she is awake.

Elizabeth's move to Chelmsford had many compensations such as when Brighid introduced her to Doug Adams, an engineer and hydraulics expert with a brilliant inventive brain. He runs his own consultative business after working in experimental departments of several famous companies. Little by little the use had been coming back to Elizabeth's neck muscles and painting was a possibility again. Perhaps Doug's engineering expertise could help the process?

'I started from scratch by making a mock-up of Elizabeth which I called "Mechanical Liz",' he told the author. 'It was a terrible waste of muscle power for her to use what few muscles she has to move the easel, so in this model I made joints in the same places as they would be in her neck. This way I could tell exactly where the movement was and how an easel would need to be planned to match in with her painting angles. At first I fixed the easel so that by means of a suck-blow device it would move backwards and forwards. I also found Mechanical Liz useful in developing the shape of the palette which had to be radial, and which I designed to suit the way her neck would turn.'

The suck-blow method was not a great success in operating the two motors which moved the easel up and down and from side to side. Undeterred, Doug decided to utilize Elizabeth's right hand which has retained a tiny amount of movement, and he inserted four micro-switches in a plastic cast. This had been moulded with careful precision by the dentist she went to in Kent — a labour of love performed in his off duty hours.

'I found that she can move the fingers of her hand slightly upwards while gravity brings them down again,' he explained. 'Her thumb is quite useful, it moves up and sideways, so there are four movements. And these are all that are needed to work the micro-switches when her hand is fitted in the cast. Because her movement is extremely light it became a question of getting the tension of the switches just so and I had to fix springs to assist them to close the circuits. To work out the exact tension I tested her finger strength by a system of pulleys and weights.

'The easel needs two reversible motors and first of all I had to work out the speed and torque on both drives, one for sideways and one for up and down. I was able to calculate the speed with a tachometer, and I measured the torque by means of a little rod with a clamp on the end, a

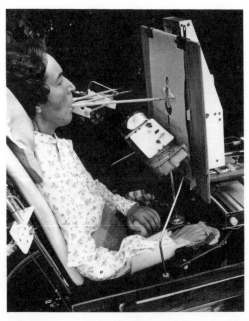

*Elizabeth using her motorised easel*

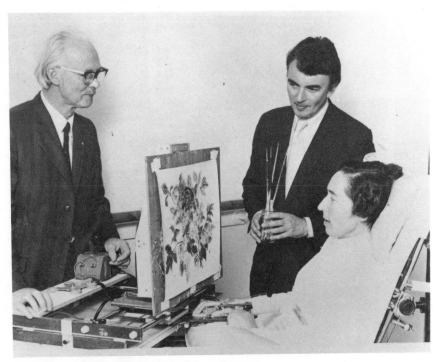

*Elizabeth with Doug Adams and actor Peter Byrne*

piece of string, a pulley and a one pound weight. I marked off the rod in inches and fitted it to the motor shaft by means of the clamp. By moving the string gradually until the weight turned the shaft round I established the pounds-inches torque required from the motor and was able to get the exact speed for the job.'

Thus, with very little finger effort, and a minimum of noise from the motors, Elizabeth can position her painting just as she requires it. Since designing this easel Doug has designed similar devices for other disabled people.

'When I work for Elizabeth I have noticed something which, as far as I am concerned, is very remarkable,' he says. 'In my workshop I hoard bits and pieces which some day may be useful, such as parts from a worn out TV set or an old camera. When I am engaged on something for her I always know beforehand that I am going to find every part I need among my bits — which does not happen when I am working for myself. Quite recently I was working on the easel when I needed a part of a certain size to fit on the end of a motor. It would have been difficult to make it because it had to fit inside one thing and outside another. Yet I went to a box of old parts and immediately found one that would fit as though it had been custom made for the job. It may sound silly but I feel it is a little bit of divine help.'

# DANCE AGAIN

To use a mouth-held paint-brush to become an internationally renowned artist was a remarkable feat, but for Elizabeth to consider returning to ballet-teaching seemed beyond the bounds of possibility. Once Roy Nash of *The Star* had infuriated her when he remarked, 'You really ought to go back to the dance, I can see you making up a ballet.'

'You're quite mad,' she retorted. 'What will you think of next!'

Later his words came back to her when she was staying at her parents' home in Kent in company with her sister Brighid's little girls. Penny, the eldest, adored her Aunt Elizabeth because once she had been a real dancer and Penny was mad about ballet.

One day when Elizabeth was on the lawn in her wheel-chair Penny came up and begged, 'Please, Auntie, give me a ballet lesson.'

There was a very strong rapport between Penny and Elizabeth and she agreed to try. As there was no music available the lesson began with Elizabeth counting and singing to give her the rhythm. Naturally Auntie was soon very flushed through lack of oxygen, but both teacher and pupil were elated. It was the first time Elizabeth had done any teaching for over a decade, while Penny was cock-a-hoop at having a lesson from someone who had actually appeared on the West End stage.

There was a world of difference between the lessons Elizabeth had given when she was physically fit and these verbal instructions accompanied by breathless counting and la-de-dahing, yet it rekindled her old interest and Penny's sessions continued on the grass. When Elizabeth planned to move to Chelmsford it was decided that Penny and her younger sister would visit her for regular instruction.

Then within a week of Elizabeth settling in her new home, Joan

*Penny*

*Doug Adams in his workshop adjusting the easel he invented for Elizabeth*

Weston, the honorary director and founder of the Chelmsford Ballet Company, asked her if she would be interested in setting a tarantella for eight girls for their forthcoming performance. Elizabeth was aghast. It was one thing to give private tuition to members of her own family, but to prepare eight strangers to perform publicly was quite another matter. Joan Weston must have had some faith in her to make the suggestion—now was the time to have faith in herself. She had never failed to meet a challenge before, and now she accepted this one—remembering Roy Nash's words as she did so.

She took her first rehearsal on the Saturday of that same week with Brighid there to make things easier for her. It seems that no one guessed just how nervous she was.

'I shall never forget how I met Elizabeth,' recalls one of the Chelmsford Ballet dancers who was involved in those early days. 'I was there for some casting auditions, and she was coming to see the dancers and choose those she wanted. At that time I knew nothing about her, except that she was a lady in a wheelchair and everybody spoke with great reverence and in hushed voices about her. "Oh, that's Miss Twistington Higgins coming . . ." And there she was. All the doors were opened wide and some of us helped to lift her wheelchair up three steps into the studio. Everybody stood around in awed silence. All the girls stopped chattering, and this very frail, thin person started to address us . . .'

And so Elizabeth returned to take an active role in the world of ballet. She may have awed the girls who were hoping for a part in her ballet but little did they guess at the tension which this outwardly composed figure was suffering. She was a strict disciplinarian and insisted that rehearsals started punctually.

But how could she express what she wanted of her students when she had no way of demonstrating the required movements? Her answer to

*The POSM indicator*

this question was given in a magazine article: 'I teach verbally. What I'm really doing is to put movements into words, trying to make people understand and do what I want. Every paralysed person knows how difficult it is trying to explain to people what to do, but it *is* possible. Not every step in dancing has a name, and often the movements need further explanation. I've simply got to get my ideas over to the dancers. It taxes my descriptive ingenuity and my pupils' powers of perception, but they are hard workers and good triers. It's a slow tedious process — exhausting for me and very frustrating on both sides. I think this is when we reach our lowest ebb.'

Despite any such low ebbs the tarantella was a great success, delighting the audience and proving to Elizabeth that she now had another creative outlet. For five years she was to be involved in the production of dances for the Chelmsford Ballet Company. In 1974, Joan Weston wrote in the May issue of *Dance,* the Journal of the Imperial Society of Teachers of Dancing: 'Since I founded the Chelmsford Ballet Company in 1947 there has been nothing to compare with the advent of Elizabeth Twistington Higgins. Her extraordinary ability and dedication under extreme handicap is quite incredible. Her indomitable spirit is reflected in the triumphant sense of achievement felt by the dancers.'

\* \* \*

'Elizabeth, I've got two very promising youngsters, and I was wondering if you would like to coach them...'

The words, amplified by the special telephone loud-speaker, filled Elizabeth's studio and she recognised the voice of Joan Weston who, as well as being the founder of the Chelmsford Ballet Company, ran the Weston School of Dancing. Apart from lessons for her two little nieces, Elizabeth had not considered giving ballet lessons on her own. For one thing, what would she do for music? When she coached dancers for the

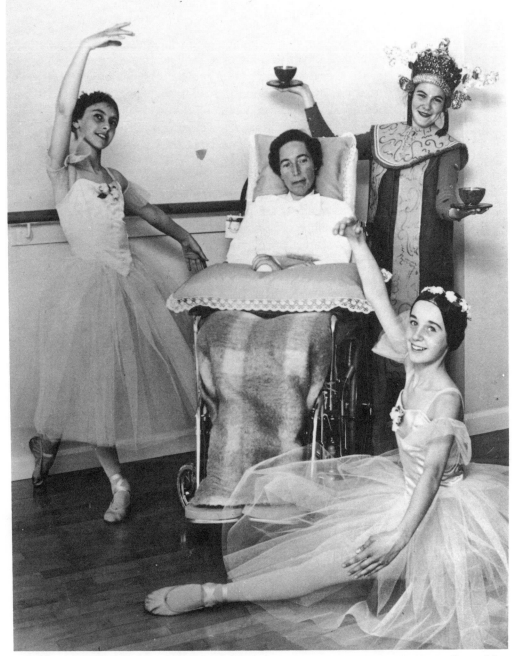

*Elizabeth with her early pupils after her return to teaching — on the left Karen Perry, Mary Buchanan — Wollaston with Linda Jones sitting*

Chelmsford Ballet Company there were always people around to assist. In her home she would be on her own. But she could not resist this challenge. She had already solved so many problems that surely the question of the music would be resolved.

'I'll try,' she told Joan. 'When can you bring them to see me?'

And so Linda Jones and Karen Perry both aged ten came into Elizabeth's life. After eighteen months of tuition Linda won a dancing scholarship to London, while nine years later Karen is a highly accomplished dancer in Elizabeth's own company, as the photographs in this book demonstrate.

The question of the music was overcome by the Possum team who had now developed a Uher tape recorder with its own control unit enabling Elizabeth to rehearse anywhere. She operated it by blowing into her mouthpiece. In this way a reel of tape could be started and stopped and, most importantly, fast wound forwards or backwards enabling her to select any part of the music she required and, if necessary, replay it over and over again while her pupils rehearsed a movement until they got it right. And in order to conserve her voice she was supplied with a battery-powered amplifier, the microphone of which was fitted to a flexible stem attached to her wheelchair.

Thanks to this unique equipment Elizabeth was able to take ballet classes and rehearsals in her own home entirely unaided. And because of the success of her lessons with Karen and Linda, she was encouraged to take on other pupils so that soon teaching assumed the same importance in her life as painting. Because nothing but the best was good enough for her girls she had the ground floor room extended into the garden to make a proper dance studio while the floor was specially sprung for ballet work.

It would be easy to think that with sophisticated controls Elizabeth's only drawback as a teacher today is that she cannot demonstrate a dance movement, but unfortunately things are rarely so straight-forward. Teaching always drains her. One of the main reasons for this is that she must concentrate on two basic things simultaneously, the rhythm of the music which accompanies the dancers' movements and the rhythm of her own breathing which depends on the conscious use of her neck muscles (known as 'frog breathing'). To appreciate how difficult this is try imagining the beat of two different tunes at the same time.

Although she has a device to amplify her voice, she still has to use her scanty breath for talking through the lesson or rehearsal. The strain of this can be imagined when one realises that her vital capacity is a mere 350cc while the normal is approximately 2,500cc. Added to these two basic difficulties is the possibility that Elizabeth may not feel well. We all know how a bad night can affect us; but a bad night in an iron lung means exhaustion the next day.

On top of physical problems there is the hassle of everyday living. Although human and electronic help enables her to maintain her busy life-style, her situation requires her to be constantly concentrating on organisation. Running her life requires more forward thinking than goes into many a small business. This includes the planning of her helpers' rotas to fit in with their needs, such as holidays or illnesses — no one with a cold should approach Elizabeth because of the dangerous effect infection can have upon her. Classes have to be arranged so that she is never too fatigued to give of her best to her pupils. There are ballet performances and art exhibitions to prepare for — it is not just painting the pictures that takes up time but arranging for them to be framed, packed and transported. Accounts have to be kept, letters replied to, bookings made and the company wardrobe maintained.

Apart from organising the chores of her twin professions, she has the responsibility of running her household, a job that is often a headache for the able-bodied.

With so much to concentrate upon Elizabeth tries to make every minute of her day count, and time lost through a break in her carefully-thought-out routine is a tragedy. A healthy person can make up a hitch in a schedule by working late or getting up early the next day, but she does not have the luxury of flexibility. The nightly discipline of the iron lung at the Broomfield Hospital dictates her hours of freedom remorselessly.

Against this busy background, Elizabeth is still able to turn her mind to creative pursuits with a mental self-discipline almost amounting to ruthlessness. But determination — like patriotism — is not enough, there has to be a wellspring of ideas.

'To plan a new ballet takes hours and hours of thought,' says Elizabeth, 'but it is the most exciting art form I know. It combines music, designing, sculpting and painting with dancing, and is endlessly stimulating. Most of my "thinking out" process is done when I lie awake at night in the iron lung. This is a time when I am most creative because I do not have to concentrate on breathing.'

*Elizabeth in the Royal Opera House, Covent Garden*

*Elizabeth watches as Gillian Toogood prepares for class. Today Gillian is a member of the Royal Swedish Ballet*

*'Pas de Quatre' finale*

# LITURGICAL BALLET

In 1971 something happened which, although Elizabeth disapproved of it at first, was to fuse her lifetime of creative experience—needlework, dancing, teaching, choreography and painting—into an utterly new and exciting whole, and was to give new meaning to her interrupted life. It came about when she was asked if she would arrange suitable dance sequences for a Holy Communion Service in Chelmsford Cathedral. This experimental form of devotion, sponsored by the Worship and Arts Association, was to be entitled *Bread of Life* and would be presented in the form of a dramatised Eucharist.

'It doesn't seem right to me to be tampering with a sacred service,' Elizabeth told the vicar who had approached her. Her paternal grandfather had been a clergyman, and she could not help smiling at the thought of what his reaction would have been to the idea of dancing in church. She must have inherited his strict attitude because she later admitted that her first reaction was one of extreme disapproval.

'Then I thought about it a great deal,' she recalls. 'As the vicar was so enthusiastic and could see nothing wrong with it, I gradually came round to the idea that if I did it the right way—if I tried to present it as another form of worship—dancing might have a place in the service. I knew that in the past dance had been used as a form of worship, and later, when I researched the subject, I realised it was Man's first way of expressing veneration. In the Bible David danced before the Ark, and all the early churches had processions and dances. Then I discovered that liturgical ballet was making a comeback in Europe today.

'In the end I agreed to try. Hopefully I created suitable movements to the music given to me—an Anthem, a *Sanctus* and a Processional hymn. The vicar wanted the dancers to wear white nylon, cassock-type dresses over white leotards. In my opinion these were rather too revealing!'

115

ehearsing for 'Lord of the Dance'

The performance in the cathedral turned out to be more moving than Elizabeth had imagined possible. Wearing their white costumes trimmed with gold, the dancers made their entrance from the West door and walked towards the altar carrying bread and wine for the communion. Each held a tall white candle, emphasising the angelic aura which seemed to surround them. Then, with true reverence, they danced to music flowing harmoniously through the cathedral. In some sequences their movements were made to the words of the service only and the effect was so beautiful it brought tears to many members of the congregation.

And what was the effect on Elizabeth while from her wheelchair, she watched the dancers weave this revived form of worship before the high altar? As a teacher of dancing whose standards start at perfection — as her pupils know only too well — her concentration was on the technique of the performance, appraising each movement which had been so carefully worked out, willing her girls to give of their best and feeling the grip of tension as they approached movements which they had found difficult in rehearsal. But as the dancing continued something transcended her practical interest; it was as though she was no longer paralysed, no longer a prisoner of wheelchair and iron-lung, but free again — and, in some mystical way — dancing again.

When the performance was over Elizabeth was left with a feeling of inner elation. Only once had she felt it so deeply before and then dancers had been floating to the music of *Les Sylphides*. In that moment she had known that come what may she was going to be a dancer. Now, three decades later in Chelmsford Cathedral, she knew that she would be devoting the rest of her life to the development of liturgical ballet. Suddenly it seemed as though everything that had happened in her life had been for a purpose.

\* \* \*

Elizabeth was not the only one whose destiny was affected by that performance. Some years later a clergyman visited her and said that at the time of her first liturgical ballet he was trying to make up his mind whether or not to go back into the Church, and it was the dancing and all it stood for which had resolved his doubts and had led to his taking orders.

'It moved me so profoundly,' he explained.

Since then many ministers have expressed surprise and delight at the effect of Elizabeth's ballet in their churches. A young curate wrote: 'It gave soul to what is basically a very dull mediaeval service — it made evensong exciting. Whereas normally we would just moan psalms at each other, it brought life and vitality. It was beautiful, it was really what worship should be: the raising of the heart and mind to God. It was not what I expected, because I've only taken part in a very simple form of liturgical dance before, which was a disaster usually because everybody gets the giggles — but this was on a different plane altogether.

'There is, I believe, a genuine part of worship in which you can participate by receiving rather than by actually moving or by singing words. I think this is the liturgical dance equivalent to the Mozart *Coronation Mass in C*. The normal Sunday evening congregation ranges between twenty and forty, but today we had one hundred and fifty.'

His enthusiasm was echoed by a parish priest in Essex who said, 'I can't express in any adequate way what we all felt after the service on Sunday morning. I had tried hard to imagine, from what my wife told me about the rehearsal here, just what we should see, but I never imagined

*A Christmas Card for the Medici Gallery*

that it would be anything so beautiful and so deeply moving as what we actually experienced. From the first moment when the girls began to proceed from the West door and then continued their graceful dancing right up to the end of *Lord of the Dance,* I felt we were all being drawn into an act of worship and praise, so full of meaning and significance, that after it none of us will ever be quite the same again.'

Dancing in church was such a revelation that invitations for Elizabeth to take the girls to other churches became so numerous that it was necessary for her to form her own group, specialising in liturgical ballet, which she named The Chelmsford Dancers. Within the next three years they made over forty appearances, and this volume of work continues.

Apart from dancing in cathedrals and churches, The Chelmsford Dancers have performed in hospitals and at charity garden fetes; they have made several television appearances and have been featured in films promoting Aid for the Disabled. When Toc H held its Diamond Jubilee at Central Hall, Westminster, Elizabeth's company was there. One of its most unusual venues was inside one of Her Majesty's Prisons.

Because of the Christian aspect of the work she is frequently asked if she regards it as an expression of gratitude to God.

'I suppose it is,' answers Elizabeth who is shy of discussing religious belief as she is sometimes expected to provide instant spiritual revelation as a product of her experiences. 'But as I don't say "Thank you, God" by producing the next ballet, it might be incidental. I do it because it is required, I do it because I love it and I do it because for me it is one of the most exciting and rewarding facets of choreography. All my life I have pioneered something. Before the polio attack I pioneered dancing classes for delicate children at Coram's Fields. When I went into the National Hospital I found myself involved in the development of the Beaverometer, and now it is liturgical dancing.

*'Bread of Life' in Chelmsford Cathedral, 1971*

117

'I find that the added work and mental stimulation which is involved in creating religious dancing — which very few people do — has led me into a lot of very interesting side-studies. For example, reading Biblical History, studying the life-style of the era, costume colouring from natural dyes, art ideas, etcetera.

'As far as the dancers are concerned I look for those with the right spiritual quality as well as a good technique. Of course they don't have to be Christians but it is much better if they have an idea of what it is all about.'

\* \* \*

'Karen... watch your front arm... one and two, one and two... weight towards your raised leg ... up, up! Good girl!' The music stops.

Elizabeth sits in her wheelchair at one end of her long studio. At the other end, opposite a mirrored wall and barre, Karen Perry pauses in her routine.

Buzz! Buzz! comes from the Possum equipment as Elizabeth controls it through her mouthpiece.

Click! The studio is filled with haunting sound again. Karen rises on her toes. Elizabeth, slightly flushed with the exertion, counts while her pupil moves gracefully through the steps to the final arabesque.

Karen, who takes lessons three times a week and has been with Elizabeth for eight years, explains that most of the time she forgets her teacher is immobilised.

'I'm more concerned with her strictness than her disability,' she says. 'I think at times she finds me stubborn, so then there is a case of strictness versus stubborness. But, of course, there is no one in the world like Elizabeth as far as I'm concerned and being in her company is very different to the Royal Ballet School where I had a year. I think here there is more emphasis on individual technique, and it is exciting to be involved in a new ballet right from the start — right from Elizabeth's first sketches. The only difficulty with her being in a wheelchair is that she cannot demonstrate what she wants us to do, but on the other hand I believe that what she has been through has given her an extra understanding which she tries to pass on to us.'

Understandably, after hundreds of lessons, Karen is used to working with a disabled teacher. What mystifies many people is how Elizabeth manages to teach the most mobile of art forms. Her assistant director, Sheila Large, a professional dancer before she came to Chelmsford and one of the original members of the group, admits that at times it is very hard going, especially when new dancers are involved.

'No matter how well taught or how classically trained, a new girl finds that she has to adapt to Elizabeth's individual style,' Sheila explains. 'But I have been with her so long that following her is second nature, and I am able to show the others exactly what she wants. To make her instructions clearer she tends to use highly descriptive terms rather than correct terminology. For example, she will say "breathe in as you pull up" — because that shows just what she wants, rather than saying "come up on to point".

'To begin with she tells you verbally what the steps are and you do them. Then she'll say "No, not like that," or "Let's try it with the other arm," until she gets what she wants. We do spend a long time getting to learn a dance, perhaps only sixteen bars in a whole Saturday's afternoon's rehearsing. On two or three occasions I have been reduced to tears because I didn't seem able to comprehend what was required.

'In her own mind she has pictured exactly how a new dance is going to look. When we actually do it we don't always come across as she imagined. Being a perfectionist, she keeps making changes until it fits in with her original concept, and some of the dancers find this annoying.

*Sheila Large*

118

And because there is something about Elizabeth which makes you forget she is paralysed, they do not appreciate her difficulties. Anything connected with dancing requires a great deal of stamina, and teaching and taking rehearsals are a strain on her. We always have the dress rehearsal a week before a performance rather than the day before because two consecutive days are too much for her.'

It is ironical that recently a new nurse remarked to Elizabeth, 'No wonder you look so young, you have never had to work.'

After all her years with The Chelmsford Dancers Sheila still finds liturgical dancing a highly emotional form of expression.

'I tend to be a rather religious person and for me it is an incredible experience,' she says. 'When four of us dance *O Salutaris* we are all very moved and this gets across to the congregation. We often notice people in tears at the end of it. Even at rehearsals one can feel suddenly touched by some aspect of the ballet. Sometimes I notice Elizabeth's eyes are rather moist.'

\* \* \*

A rocket!

There are usually eight members of Elizabeth's Chelmsford Dancers, three of whom have been with the group since 1971. These stalwarts have been invaluable in helping to integrate new dancers recruited to replace other members of the company who have left for new careers in hospitals, universities or to dance professionally on the stage. Ex-members are frequently welcomed back to the group in between their engagements. The dancers perform for the love of it, their only remuneration being for travelling expenses. These can be a drain on the company's finances as several professional dancers travel from London regularly for the Saturday afternoon rehearsals. Elizabeth is adamant that her dancers must be of a high standard and this means recruiting them from outside her area.

The modest fee paid by churches to the company for a performance often does not cover the expenses of mounting it, and ways of raising money have included a fete held in Elizabeth's garden which was a success despite the fact it turned out to be the wettest day of the year. One suspects that when funds get dangerously low she gets to work at her easel. Generous assistance for the company comes from local firms, from a London wig-maker and from Moss Bros who sent the Dancers a number of their hire wedding dresses for which they had no further use. Elizabeth, with her passion for needlework, saw they could be modified into excellent costumes.

Her visualization of what the dancers should wear comes at the same time as a new ballet begins to form in her mind. She will use her brush and paints to sketch them, and then Ann Perry, Karen's mother, various helpers and Sheila begin dyeing, cutting out and stitching.

'This is an aspect I thoroughly enjoy,' Elizabeth says. 'There are not many choreographers who design their own costumes. I am lucky to be able to put down on paper what I want and then supervise the making of them right through. I could only manage this through the quick understanding of Sheila Large and her expert knowledge of sewing and dancing. Together we have spent hours creating a really lovely wardrobe.

'I know from experience that a dancer performs better if she is aware that she is beautifully dressed. The long hours of work spent in this house on the creation and care of the costumes account for a large percentage of the company's success.

'The whole essence of our wardrobe has been "nipping, cutting and contriving", but for me it is a continuation that dates back to the nursery with Nanny's ragbag, the war intervening, insufficient material so that

*Above, costume design for
'O Salutaris Hostia' and right,
the actual performance*

one had to make do with old parachutes and coupon-free material and limited funds for the Penny Concerts. It was always a case of necessity being the mother of improvisation, and often the improvised costumes turn out very satisfactorily in spite of drastic mistakes. For instance when I designed the costumes for *The Magnificat* I decided to try and re-create the kind of colouring that would have been available in Biblical times using natural dyes or hand-woven linen. We used unbleached calico and the skirts, which were to have been terra-cotta, turned out a soft rose pink. This proved to be a most harmonious combination with brown, saffron and pale blue. As Doug Adams would say..."a little bit of divine help."

'The inspiration for my ideas has involved me in some fascinating research and I am often influenced by stained glass windows, the symbolic ritual of the liturgy and religious paintings. People who have seen our *Dei Gloria* will recognise the costumes as pure Botticelli. The local library has been most helpful in supplying me with endless reference books. I am always open to suggestion, especially to special requests from members of the clergy.

'I have a favourite madonna in one of the little chapels at Tewkesbury Abbey, and one day I am going to build a ballet around her. She is dressed in delicate pink and green and she is already in a dancing pose, kneeling behind her baby.'

The process of creating a new ballet begins with Elizabeth listening to a lot of music. In her search for the right sort she has her radio tuned to Radio 3 continuously. When she has decided on the pieces she wants

*Sewing afternoon as the costumes are prepared*

she has them recorded and then plays them over and over again while she begins to visualize the dance movements.

'I have my arm slung up for typing out the choreograph, and that is pretty hard work because I might be working on eight parts simultaneously,' she explains. 'I think and think and think and lose myself in the music which I usually play over more than a hundred times, but if it is a really good piece I never tire of listening to it.

'Teaching is the hardest part of a new ballet. Often we really reach rock bottom because I tend to get exasperated when I can't explain it well enough. Then it jells, and suddenly everything becomes very exciting for all concerned.

'What the public does not realise is the amount of team work that goes on backstage. A finished performance looks so easy and gives no hint of the multitudinous things that it depends upon. Apart from the dancers, many people are involved including my helpers and drivers. Without them nothing could be done and all my work reflects their enthusiasm.'

When The Chelmsford Dancers are invited to a church Elizabeth and Sheila visit it to measure out the actual dancing area. This varies in every case and the dance has to be adapted to fit within the dimensions available. The surface on which the performance will take place often causes anxiety. After practising on the specially sprung floor, a dancer could easily damage a foot or leg through landing too heavily on unyielding stone. On the day of one performance it was found that a wooden floor had been so thoroughly waxed it was only by sprinkling it with sticky Coca-Cola that it became safe to dance upon. An inevitable headache is working out how the performers can make graceful entrances and exits in buildings designed for traditional ritual rather than dance routines.

At dress rehearsals Elizabeth's audio expert Malcolm Salmon experiments with his speakers to get the best acoustic effects. Not only does he provide sound for the company's performances, but he spends uncounted hours making master tapes from the versions Elizabeth edits

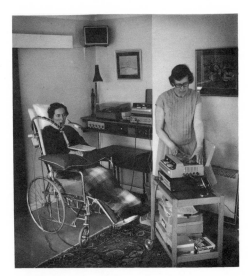

*Elizabeth Trellis helping Elizabeth with reel to reel recorder for rehearsal tape*

121

*Brighid sprinkling lemonade on the floor for the Chelmsford Dancers television debut for BBC 1 in 1974*

on her three Possum-controlled tape recorders. Like all the others, his sole reward is the satisfaction of seeing a ballet produced.

Of the many compositions in the repertoire of The Chelmsford Dancers the *Ballet of the Church Seasons* has been the most popular, perhaps because it is quintessential of liturgical dance. Elizabeth based it on Mozart's *Laudate Dominum* from *Vespare Solemnis* and his *Credo-et Incarnatus Est* from the *C Minor Mass*. In it Elizabeth succeeded in conveying, through the symbolic colours of the costumes, the order of the Church Calendar and the mood of each season — violet for Advent and Lent, gold for the Festivals, red for Whitsun, green for Trinity, and blue for the Virgin Mary. The synopsis reads: 'Advent heralds the Birth of Christ, followed by the penitential season of Lent and the agony of the Crucifixion. Then Easter brings the sudden realisation and wonder of the Resurrection; Whitsun — the Holy Spirit, and Trinity the hope and joy of the Christian life.'

It is a taxing theme for five dancers to portray, but it was this ballet which was shown by the BBC in a *Seeing and Believing* television programme in 1974.

Commenting on this ballet, the Bishop of Chelmsford wrote: 'I was pretty sceptical when I heard of liturgical dance and I feared the worst. In the event I was moved beyond words when, in the Cathedral, I first saw the *Ballet of the Seasons of the Church's Year*. It was a most beautiful expression of worship, faith and joy... The Christian life seems so often to the outsider to be cold and joyless. We need to show our joy through our bodies as well as our voices.'

The next year Elizabeth's dancers performed at Chelmsford maximum security prison. She was warned that a prison audience can be the toughest in the world, and at Chelmsford the 'appreciation' received by some previous entertainers ranged from mild abuse to the throwing of benches. What would be the reaction of men serving long sentences to classical ballet, national and liturgical dancing?

A lucky accident created a responsive atmosphere. After the first few steps of the opening Spanish dance a petticoat slipped to the floor. The

122

*Visit to prison for a performance. On the right, two of the lads help Elizabeth inside. On the left, Susan Mitchell and Sheila Large prepare for the show*

*Rehearsal in prison*

men—hoping it was the beginning of a striptease—cheered and stamped while the dancer coolly stepped out of the garment, kicked it to one side and carried on. The ice was broken and the exit was made to thunderous applause.

After the performance one of the inmates went to his cell and returned with a gift which he laid on Elizabeth's lap—a beautifully carved model of a gypsy caravan which now graces her studio. It was his way of expressing his thanks. One of his mates said, 'I came here really to have a laugh and a joke and more or less throw abuse around, but I was stunned, I was really stunned by the whole performance.'

'I think my colleagues'd sooner look at the girls than the Governor—definitely,' commented another. A third was recorded saying, 'Some people have a lot more strength than others. Some go under in a crisis, but she's found an inner strength. You meet people like that in prison. They either go under or they fight to survive and achieve something in this life and don't look back on what's actually happened to them. And that's exactly what that woman has done. Now she's teaching and giving that gift to young people, what she didn't achieve in her own life. She's probably looking at the girls she trains and seeing a bit of herself in them. Perhaps she'll create a star—a ballerina—and then she'll probably feel that she's achieved the greatest thing in her life.'

*Elizabeth Twistington Higgins MBE with Dame Ninette de Valois at a preview of the film* The Dance Goes On

124

*In the ruins of Coventry Cathedral*

# THE AIDIS TRUST

'What is the worst aspect of your life?'

This question was asked by an interviewer recording Elizabeth for Education Audio-Cassettes on the subject of 'Stress-Living with a Serious Physical Handicap'.

'Monotony,' came the quick reply. 'Knowing that vital nursing procedures are going on forever, unlike most people who, going into hospital, know that within two or three weeks they will be out again. The nightly choreography of being put into an iron lung is rigidly boring but to keep one's bodily functions on an even keel one must stick to some form of routine. You must eat and drink at definite times and this, too, tends to get monotonous.'

Elizabeth's day...

6.30 a.m.: Nurses lift her out of the iron lung at Broomfield Hospital. They wash her and clean her teeth, dress her, feed her breakfast and set her in her wheelchair.

8.30 a.m.: Her driver arrives with her ambulance and her chair is wheeled into it.

8.45 a.m.: The ambulance arrives at her home where a helper is already waiting. The equipment she requires has been set up in readiness the night before so she can start work immediately, usually painting or teaching.

11.30 a.m.: By now Elizabeth is tired of sitting up and her wheelchair is set to the prone position in which she finds it easier to breathe.

12.00 a.m.: Her helper feeds her lunch after which she reads or, if working on a new ballet, listens to music.

2.15 p.m.: Changeover of helpers.

3.30 p.m.: After working again Elizabeth rests in the horizontal position—unless she is rehearsing in which case she carries on upright.

5.30 p.m.: The helper prepares Elizabeth for supper.

5.45 p.m.: Supper.

6.00 p.m.: Elizabeth makes her long-distance telephone calls and prepares her work for the morning so she can start it while she is still fresh.

7.15 p.m.: The ambulance takes her back to Broomfield Hospital.

7.30 p.m.: Two nurses begin the two-hour ritual of preparing her for bed. As it is a teaching hospital she often finds herself instructing a new nurse in the operation of the iron lung.

9.30 p.m.: Now in the breathing machine, Elizabeth is 'clamped down' for the night.

Day after day, seven days a week, this routine does not vary except when Elizabeth travels to a performance or is able to make highly complicated arrangements for going on holiday.

Over the past few years a cherished break from this monotony is an annual visit to the beautiful Cotswold village of Broadway. It began as a result of her painting and became a very important aspect of her ballet work.

In 1974 the Padre of Toc H, Bob Knight, asked if Elizabeth could arrange for the Mouth and Foot Painting artists to give an exhibition of their work at the Cotswold Festival to be held at Broadway the following year, and would she make a personal appearance painting at her easel? She replied that she was sure an exhibition could be arranged, but to the latter question her answer was an emphatic 'No', though she added she would be happy to visit the exhibition and chat informally to visitors. She suggested it might be a good idea to make a trial visit to Broadway that year—if a place could be found for her to stay with the iron lung—so everything would go smoothly in 1975.

'Toc H never does things by half,' says Elizabeth. 'Within a week Bob wrote back saying he'd found a house where the owner, an elderly gentleman, would be willing for me to have his dining room. My sisters Janet and Brighid went to Broadway on an advance visit. They had been told that the house was by the church. When they located it they found it had a great flight of steps, making it totally inaccessible for me and my heavy equipment.

'"That might not be The Court," said Brighid who is an optimist. Sure enough, they found another church at the far end of the village and beside it a magnificent Elizabethan house with only three steps down. Though unnamed, it turned out to be The Court.

'They found the owner to be a charming gentleman named Richard Ayshford-Sanford who, since his wife's death, had lived alone with two white cats, Minnie and Moppy. They reigned supreme, living off the fat of the land. This quiet thoughtful man was proposing to put his dining room with its crystal chandelier, beautiful antique furniture and Persian carpet at my disposal. My sisters were appalled. They explained that the iron lung was an absolute monster and, among other dreadful things, it dripped oil everywhere.

'"That's all right," he said. "Will she want to go out in it every day?" Janet and Brighid found it hard to remain straight-faced at this question knowing what a struggle it would be just to get it in and out of the house just once. They proceeded to paint as black a picture as possible, but Richard made light of everything and refused to be put off. When it came to the question of how much would he charge. . .

'"Nothing," he answered simply and the arrangements were finalised

*The Occasional Singers provide an interlude to Elizabeth's choreography at Therfield, Hertfordshire*

with a piercing "mieow" from one of the cats. Hearing about this momentous meeting and how my problems had been firmly and politely brushed aside, I realised I had been unbelievably lucky.

'"Typical Elizabeth," said Janet. "Always falls on her feet!"'

Elizabeth had a splendid holiday, spending some of the time paving the way for the MFPA exhibition to be held the following year. Richard was most helpful, making arrangements for her to meet various members of the Festival Committee, either at the Court or 'up at the Knap'. The Knap was the pet name for Dor Knap (Anglo Saxon words meaning 'the little house under the hill'). It had once been part of his family's estate, but was now a much used meeting place for Toc H.

"To reach this eyrie, we had to drive up the bumpiest track imaginable, slowly zig-zagging up the side of a very steep hill," Elizabeth recalls. The final destination was worth every jolt. The view was breath-taking... a fantastic panorama of the surrounding country-side. There was a conference centre, a delightful little chapel converted from an old stable, and a new recreation room in which the art exhibition would be held. All this had been reconstructed and built up gradually during the years by willing volunteers which no doubt accounted for some of its unique atmosphere. This was to be the focal point for the Cotswold Festival and people from all over the country would be gathering there to enjoy the weekend.

'Richard, his family and his staff were most friendly and hospitable, going out of their way to give me an enjoyable rest. I'm afraid Brighid, my two nurses and myself literally "took over" the Court, but whatever Richard felt about our "invasion", he appeared to accept it with philosophic equanimity. To my mind, he's one in a million — for this was to be the first of several such visits!' On the last day she sat in the garden in her wheelchair looking at an enormous yew hedge with an archway in the middle which she felt would make a superb backdrop.

'You know, Richard, your garden would make the most perfect setting for a ballet,' she said but her remark was greeted by silence and she though that perhaps she had been presumptious. But she had not been back in Chelmsford for more than a few days when a letter arrived from Richard saying he had put the idea for a ballet in his garden to the festival committee and they accepted it enthusiastically.

At the Toc H Cotswold Festival held in September, 1975, over forty paintings were exhibited by Mouth and Foot Painting artists and Erich Stegmann flew from Germany to give the demonstration which Elizabeth had declined. The Chelmsford Dancers opened the festival with a group of musicians known as The Occasional Singers and in *An Evening of Ballet, Madrigals and Wine,* and the weekend ended with a liturgical ballet during Evensong in the lovely old Anglo-Saxon church of St Eadburgha. So popular were these performances that Elizabeth's dancers were invited back to Broadway the following year.

Perhaps the most important thing to come out of it for Elizabeth was an association with The Occasional Singers, a group of amateur and professional musicians who make music for the joy of it, led by John Hull, the Artistic Director for Toc H. Since then the dancers and the Singers have frequently joined forces to present a performance, while John Hull has written music for Elizabeth to choreograph, the most notable being for a BBC television production *Pleasure as Praise* in the *Meeting Place* series. She greatly values the collaboration, saying, 'We love working with the Toc H people... I don't know whether it's because they are excessively friendly or that they have the right attitude to life, but they are extremely jolly and it is one big laugh all the time with them.'

*Bob Knight*

*Richard Ayshford-Sanford*

* * *

The Chelmsford Dancers at St Eadburgha's Church, Broadway, Worcestershire

Elizabeth is associated with one other Christian-inspired organisation, The Aidis Trust. This should not be taken to mean that she is any way 'holy' — her personal beliefs are too down-to-earth for that, and her brand of Christianity has been aptly described as astringent.

The Aidis Trust was founded in 1975 to help disabled and elderly people by sponsoring urgently needed electronic equipment. Today the President is HRH the Duke of Edinburgh, and among its distinguished list of vice-presidents is Jacqueline du Pré and Group Captain Leonard Cheshire VC. It was felt that too often organisations to benefit incapacitated people had been set up by well-intentioned people without any real conception of what handicap is all about, so it was a fundamental decision that Aidis should have a handicapped person as a trustee because of their experience.

'Elizabeth giving her name and encouragement at the start of Aidis as a well-known handicapped person was the most important thing in its establishment,' says one of the Trust's founders. 'Many, many others have been encouraged by her to lead more meaningful lives.'

One of the most significant aspects of the work of the Aidis Trust is its Toyaids project. It was started for the benefit of children who are deprived of normal play because they are severely disabled, often not being able to move their hands or arms. Under the direction of Peter Toft, at the Engineering Centre for Special Schools in Woolwich College, adaptions are made to conventional toys so that by the slightest nudge on a control panel disabled children can use a toy unaided. These adaptions are undertaken at the college by handicapped people who derive much pleasure from the fact that they are helping children with similar problems to their own.

130

*Elizabeth with disabled child*

It is almost impossible to describe the delight expressed by severely disabled children when for the first time in their lives they are able to control toys similar to those that physically fit children enjoy. Thanks to Toyaids they receive untold pleasure and with it a reassurance they have not experienced before, and at the same time they are being prepared to use the equipment upon which they will depend later in life.

The Aidis Trust makes its Toyaids available to hospitals, schools and centres for the handicapped, toy libraries and members of the general public all over the world.

*Handicapped group working at the Ashley Centre*

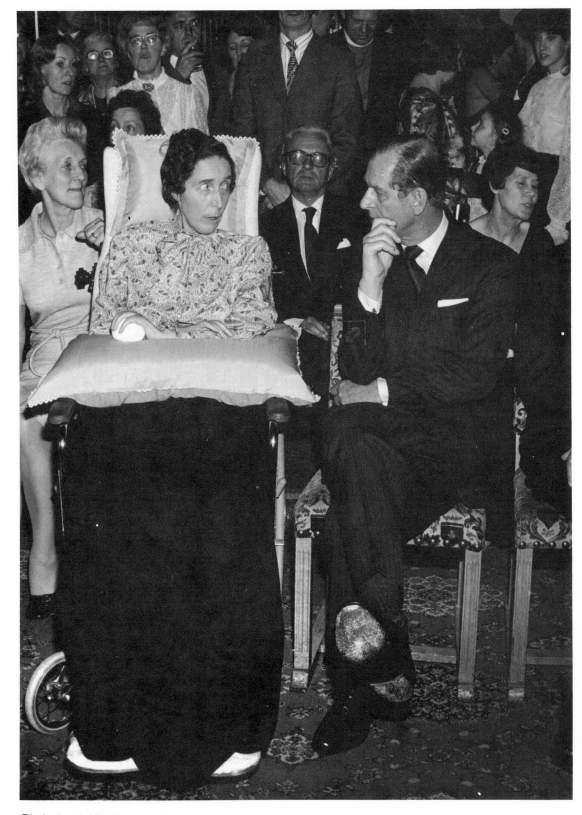

*Elizabeth with HRH Prince Philip, Duke of Edinburgh*

# ROYAL COMMAND

On November 24, 1976, the sharp eyes of Elizabeth caught sight of one of the letters that was being opened for her. It was marked FROM THE PRIME MINISTER IN CONFIDENCE, and without batting an eyelid she said to her helper, 'You can put that to one side, I'll read it later. The next one is the one I have been waiting for.' As soon as she was alone Elizabeth telephoned Betty who does secretarial work for her.

'I don't want to be a nuisance, but how soon could you come up and see me,' she asked. 'Something important has to be dealt with, but I would rather not talk about it over the phone.'

When Betty arrived, clearly intrigued by the excitement in her friend's voice, she held up the letter so she could read it. The first paragraph stated: 'Madam, The Prime Minister has asked me to inform you, in strict confidence, that he has it in mind, on the occasion of the forthcoming list of New Year Honours, to submit your name to The Queen with a recommendation that Her Majesty may be graciously pleased to approve that you be appointed a Member of the Order of the British Empire.'

A form expressing acceptance had to be signed and returned to Downing Street.

'I was so surprised and excited that when I took the brush in my mouth to draw my signature I made a terrible botch of it,' Elizabeth says. 'I don't know what the officials must have thought when they saw it. I asked Betty to enclose a note of apology and explanation.'

Now the problem was to keep the news of the honour a secret until the New Year when the list would be officially published. It would have been so delightfully easy to give a hint to members of her family or to her devoted helpers, but Elizabeth managed to resist the temptation and so did Betty.

Because January 1, 1977, fell on a Saturday, the Honours' List was published on December 31.

'Apparently I was mentioned on Radio London but there was no mention of my award on Radio 4 to which I was listening,' says Elizabeth. 'I even began to wonder if I had imagined the whole thing, and it wasn't until the newspaper man did his round of the hospital and I saw the announcement of the award on the front page of the local paper that I knew it was really true. I could not help feeling very moved by the delighted congratulations of all the staff. But at home things fell rather flat. I had expected to be interrupted all morning with telephone calls but in actual fact only three or four people rang me. I waited in vain to hear from the family and in desperation phoned them in the evening. They were flabbergasted and most apologetic that they had not noticed my name in the list.'

Elizabeth's investiture was to be held in February with the Duke of Kent officiating but the weather was so bad that her doctor suggested

*Elisabeth Swan*

*Gillian Toogood*

*Karen Perry*

*Susan Mitchell*

*Denise Barber*

*Lynne Hutchings*

she should try to go at a later date. When she rang Buckingham Palace to ask if it could be postponed she found the officials delightfully friendly and helpful. A list of seven alternative dates was read out to her but she had an understandable wish to receive the award from the Queen's own hand. As it was Jubilee Year Her Majesty would not be free to hold an investiture until July and with great diffidence Elizabeth asked if she could wait until then.

'Of course,' said the Palace official. 'Whatever you like. Would July 20 be convenient?'

The delay gave Elizabeth plenty of time to plan her outfit. She went on a shopping spree to buy materials for a blouse which would not clash with the rose pink ribbon of the Order, and for some pillowslips which would tone in with both. Normally she found shopping a tiresome chore which she would gladly leave to others but the owner of the shop, and his assistants, were immensely helpful and turned this outing into an enjoyable social afternoon.

Iris Rose, one of the nurses who looks after Elizabeth at Broomfield Hospital, is also a talented needlewoman and usually makes most of Elizabeth's clothes. This blouse had to be just right as it was to make a royal debut.

The investiture was to be held at 11am which meant that the recipients and their guests had to be in their places about half an hour before the ceremony started. Iris arrived to get Elizabeth out of the iron lung soon after 5 o'clock, and she was able to leave the hospital promptly at seven.

'Two nurses were to accompany me — Anne drove the ambulance with its special sticker on the windscreen, picking Betty up on the way,' says Elizabeth. 'Once in London we threaded through ever-thickening traffic until Coram's Fields was reached. The secretary there had thoughtfully left everything ready for our reception — tea, coffee, milk and a kettle. It was lovely to have this brief respite. Coram playground was deserted at this hour, a tranquil oasis in the midst of a busy city.

'Normally a recipient is only allowed to take two guests, but in my case the rules were waived. My sisters Janet and Brighid met us there and excitement mounted as we drove along the Mall and joined the line of taxis and cars which was being directed through the gates of Buckingham Palace. Police escorted my ambulance across the courtyard to a door on the left of the building where I was unloaded and carried up the steps by two members of the palace staff.

'We waited in the vestibule for the return of an elegant mahogany lift which had just made a sedate take-off filled with some elderly and preoccupied passengers who were presumably unable to climb the stairs. Time seemed to drag until it returned, then a gentle ride upwards and my wheelchair was taken out and pushed smartly along a very long corridor. In no time at all I had lost my bearings and the morning adventure developed a feeling of unreality.

'I was rolled across the back of the ballroom and a swift glance to my right showed me a vast, high-ceilinged room, lit by sparkling chandeliers. At the far end were two great thrones surmounted by golden crowns from which streamed long red velvet curtains. It was a veritable fairytale ballroom and could have been the setting for Act III of *Swan Lake* or the prologue for *Sleeping Beauty.* Background music was provided by the Guards' Band while the hundred and ninety recipients were prepared for the ceremony.

'I was propelled swiftly onwards to an anteroom beyond, coming to a halt by a couch at the far end on which sat a lonely figure. One of the pages introduced him and we saw that the man was blind. We tried hard to put into words the scene we had just glimpsed and kept him informed to the best of our ability as to what was happening around us. There was

*Filming for 'The Light of Experience'*

one other lady, who was slightly lame, waiting with us. All of us were to receive the M.B.E. and we were lucky because only twenty-five feet away was the royal dias.

'We had a funny session to begin with. I had on a blouse which opened at the back but which had buttons down the front to appear as though it fastened in the usual way. An official came along with a little hook, which he wanted to pin on the blouse so that the insignia could be easily hung on it when the time came. He was fooled by the buttons and could not get it in place so Brighid said, "I'll do it for you," but when she tried to unbutton me she was also deceived by the false buttons. Then she took a fold of the material and told the official to fix to that, whereupon he promptly ran the sharp pin into her finger.

Elizabeth saw that while the guests remained in the ballroom, the recipients were placed in different anterooms leading off it according to the orders they were to receive.

And then it was the moment she had dreamed of for months.

'Elizabeth Twistington Higgins!'

As her name was called the page pushed the wheelchair forward, turned at the exact spot and wheeled Elizabeth before her sovereign. The Queen stepped down from the dais and deftly placed the order on the little hook which had given so much trouble earlier on.

'Her Majesty is very petite, being little higher than I was sitting in my wheelchair,' says Elizabeth. 'Her voice was soft and melodious, and she seemed to generate kindliness. And how well she must have done her homework. That morning nearly two hundred people came before her and only the name of the recipient was announced with no hint as to what they were being honoured for. Yet Her Majesty had words for everybody, and when it was my turn she had a long talk to me about my painting.

'Then, by way of dismissal, she said, "I do hope this outing has not tired

135

you too much." The page took control of the wheelchair and I was rolled away, a Member of the British Empire.

'As I left the ballroom some official offered me his congratulations as he removed my medal and handed it to a second official who placed it in a special case. This was then handed to me but I had to ask twice if he would mind laying it on my lap. He had not noticed that I could not move my hands. I was then pushed round so that I could enter the back of the hall and watch the remainder of the investiture.

'Things had been so beautifully organised that my party was reunited and the blind man was still with us. Brighid helped him to feel his medal and again tried to describe the scene for him. How sad to think that he could only sense the atmosphere and hear the music played quietly by the Guards' Band in the minstrels' gallery. How thankful I was that I could examine in detail the whole enchanting setting, the grandeur of the occasion, the paintings on the walls, the predominating colours of red and gold. It was exactly as one had always imagined a palace ballroom to be.

'Deep down I knew that I wouldn't have got the MBE for painting as I never would have painted if I hadn't got polio... What I do feel very strongly is that my award was a shared one. Without my helpers, mentors and incredible luck in finding inventors such as Doug and unsung others such as dental mechanics, firms who've bent their rules, volunteers who've done countless mucky jobs, the Mouth and Foot Artists — none of my efforts could have materialised without their endless and continuous assistance and encouragement.'

*At St Eadburgha's Church, Broadway*

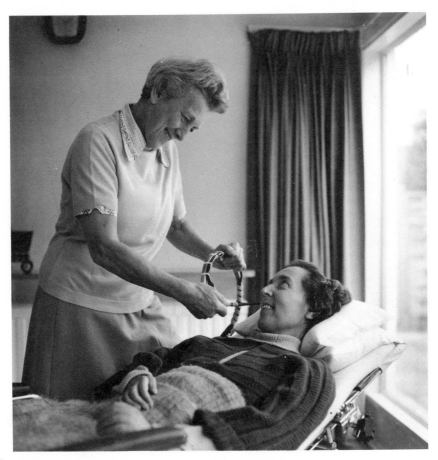

*Peggy Lomas fixing
Elizabeth to her lifeline*

*Sheila Large and Gillian Bruce — 'Low at His Feet*

# EPILOGUE

Twenty-six years have gone by since poliomylitis struck Elizabeth that hot summer day in 1953. Since then we have seen how she has struggled for survival as a physical being and as an artist. At first the fight was instinctive, then conscious and then it was a battle with the result that she has achieved things that in the early days of her illness would have seemed utterly impossible — the independence provided by her Chelmsford home, worldwide recognition as a painter and her own company of dancers.

With all this experience behind her, what does she now feel about her life? After the year-long series of interviews on which this book is based, the author sought to find out by asking these seven questions: —

*Elizabeth, do you feel that you have accepted your situation?*

I hope that I have come to terms with, and accepted, the extent of my paralysis, and I have tried hard to use to the full the few muscles that still function. If you are asking me whether I am satisfied with my way of life my answer would be No! My working hours are far too short though stamina-wise I doubt if I could cope with a longer working day and although I know that certain nursing procedures are vital, I begrudge the six hours it takes performing them. It is a large chunk out of a fourteen-hour day.

Living at home would probably relieve some of the pressures and tensions caused by the lifestyle of a commuter but too many problems bar the way to this dream at present.

My body is sometimes a burden and always a considerable responsibility to many, but only on very rare occasions am I made to feel this is so. The nightly hospitality, medical and nursing care that I receive from the staff at Broomfield Hospital, the knowledge that my life support equipment is serviced regularly there and that an emergency generator would take over if the electricity fails, is enormously reassuring. These arrangements, made before I moved to Chelmsford, combined with my rota of loyal helpers, have enabled me to 'live' again. My interesting and very varied work schedule has only been made possible by the constant and dedicated assistance of all concerned.

*What do you miss most now?*

The sense of touch. Many people think that because I am paralysed my body is numb but as the polio virus does not attack sensory nerves I can still feel. The residual paralysis is determined by the number of motor nerves killed off during the acute stage of the illness. These are the nerves which relay the messages from the brain to the muscles and if they are dead there is no possible chance of that muscle moving.

I am often asked what it feels like to be paralysed. Apart from being unable to move which causes considerable discomfort, and the non-stop battle to breathe, my body feels normal. If I could be granted three wishes I would choose the return of my diaphragm, my hands and my arms.

I long to cuddle babies, fondle the family pets, and enjoy the feel of sculptures or the texture of pottery, materials and other everyday objects. My sister has a most gorgeous puppy who cannot understand why I am the only one who doesn't pick him up — and how I would love to. But perhaps, above all, I would like to shake hands with people. So often someone makes a move to do so and, realising I cannot reciprocate, snatches away their hands. This used to upset me but now I'm tougher and I accept it as a compliment because they have ignored my handicap. To save their embarrassment I usually say, 'Oh I know it's a funny hand but go on, shake it.' The trouble is then that they give you a great whamming shake which can be rather painful.

*What have you learned through your experience?*

Though much has been taken from me, much has been given in return and I have found that being confined to a wheelchair can have compensations. Most people are intrinsically kind and I am constantly receiving surprisingly generous help from various sources.

There are a few people with sadistic tendencies who appear to enjoy their powerful hold over us. But fortunately the balance drops firmly away from this type of person and falls more often towards those who make life bearable and work possible.

I think that the caring, compassionate, loving human being possesses the greatest of all God's gifts. And I have learned that loyalty can never be repaid and dedication cannot be purchased with money.

During my long years of rehabilitation people frequently said to me, 'You ought to do this or that because so-and-so did it.' Their suggestions, though well intended, used to exasperate me so I try never to force my own ideas on handicapped colleagues. If I can I will happily offer practical advice and try to put them in touch with the right sort of help, especially regarding equipment, but I refuse to tell them what they *ought* to do. Everyone's circumstances are different and we can never know their complete story.

In my opinion it is vital that we should be allowed to do things in our own time and not when other people tell us that we should.

*In the light of that, what would you say to a handicapped person?*

It is absolutely necessary to maintain a sense of humour even if it is a slightly pawky one like mine and not always appreciated. We have to face the fact that, whether we like it or not, we are a captive audience, so, if you have the time and the inclination you will have the satisfaction of knowing that you are giving a very useful service to others. Today people automatically say 'How are you?' but only a few really want an honest reply. However, many obviously do need a ready ear for their own personal problems.

Try to accept your handicap and the ensuing difficulties and concentrate on what you have left. It is surprising how many things are possible (those that seem impossible may take a little longer) especially if you refuse to take 'no' for an answer. Don't be afraid to ask, nag if necessary, fight if you are driven to do so — but *never* give in. Even if it makes you unpopular your persistence may help others as well as yourself.

Bureaucratic restrictions can be extremely frustrating and at times seem to have been designed to discourage us at every turn. One cannot help feeling that the tedious months of waiting for vital necessities, such as a wheelchair or special equipment with which to work, could be

*A moment of relaxation*

drastically reduced and the maintenance services for these things improved.

It is not surprising that some people are brought to the brink of despair and many take the line of least resistance and opt out. Every citizen in this country has a right to work and to live to the full. Disabled people are no exception and there must be many who, given the necessary encouragement and help, could become useful members of society. Probably they will know only too well that 'it is more blessed to give than to receive'.

*What is the most important aspect of your life?*

My work. I simply cannot envisage living without it. The urge to create, whether on canvas or with dancing, is still strong and has to be released. This is why working with The Chelmsford Dancers is such a great incentive; choreography to suit their individual talents is a challenge, stretching my ability to the full. Often feelings of panic over-whelm me when I realise that I am not being as original as I want to be, but inspiration is a frighteningly elusive gift. It does not arrive on demand. And it may be months of dreary slogging before an idea suddenly flashes across my mind, obtained inexplicably from some totally unexpected source. It is as though an enormous weight has been lifted from me and I feel exhilarated.

I shall be happy as long as I am able to go on with my work because I like to feel that I am not taking all the time — and I like to earn my own money.

*After all that you have experienced, do you believe there is an after-life?*

Most certainly. I think that our brief time on earth would be quite pointless if it ended with death. I am sure I shall meet again the many wonderful people I have known during my life. Without my belief in the resurrection, and the hope it inspires in the hearts of Christians everywhere, I would be unable to choreograph liturgical dancing with any sincerity.

These ballets are the most eloquent way I have of expressing my faith.

*And what do you think of as your ultimate goal?*

I should think a nice little dance in heaven.

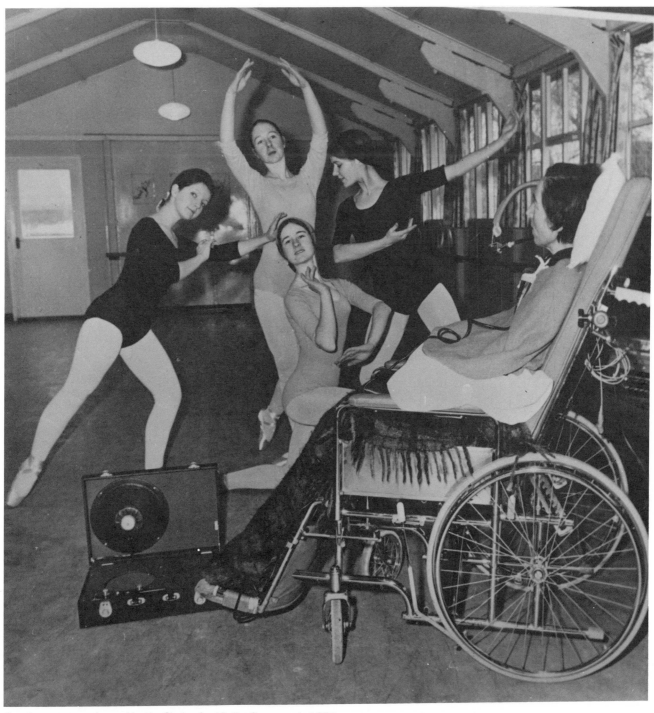

*Pas de quatre—a rehearsal by the Chelmsford Ballet Company in 1970*